An Introduction to

Old Order *and* Conservative Mennonite Groups

D0061886

An Introduction to

Old Order *and* Conservative Mennonite Groups

Stephen Scott

People's Place Book #12

Good Books

Intercourse, PA 17534

Acknowledgements

The many faceted story of the Old Order and Conservative Mennonites contained in this book is to a large extent based on a long interest in these people and on more than 25 years of contact with members of the various groups. Many individuals among both the Old Order and Conservative groups gave much help and encouragement to complete this project. Special thanks are due to those who willingly gave their valuable assistance.

Amos B. Hoover shared his considerable knowledge of Old Order Mennonite life and history, including the Stauffer Mennonites. Mabel Burkholder also contributed much information concerning the Old Order Mennonites. Edsel Burdge Jr. provided insights and information on the Conservative Mennonite Movement, especially the groups in the Cumberland Valley of Pennsylvania and Maryland. Steven Nolt gave much help in interpreting 19th and 20th century Mennonite Church history. These four people as well as John Hartzler of Christian Light Publications and James Boll of Rod and Staff Publishers kindly reviewed the text and gave many helpful suggestions.

Several dozen other individuals through personal interviews, correspondence and telephone conversations provided large and small pieces of information to make the Old Order and Conservative Mennonite story more complete. These individuals are listed alphabetically according to the group of which they spoke. Old Order Mennonites who use horses and buggies: Karsten Albertsen, David and Alta Hoover, Isaac Horst, Lewis Martin, John Rhodes, and Elva Royer. Car-driving Old Order Mennonites: Clare Frey, Melvin Huber, Amos Martin, Donald Martin, David Miller, Lester Sauder, Harvey and Mabel Weaver and Lloyd Weiler. Stauffer Mennonites: Ezra Martin and Enos Stauffer. Reformed Mennonites: Alan Keyser. Conservative Mennonite Movement: Mervin Baer, William Bear, Chris Beiler, Tom Bender, Geroge R. Brunk II, Eby Burkholder, Lester Burkholder, Roy Geigley, Clarence Gerig, Aden Gingerich, Raymond Harnish, Jerry Helmuth, Earl Horst, Fred Hostetler, Lydia (Mrs. Sam) Kanagy, Arlen Krabill, Russel Krabill, Wilbur Kropf, Nelson Kurtz, James Landis, Paul Landis, James and Mattie Lowry, Ivan Martin Jr., Fred Nighswander, Elvin Rohrer, Ray Shaum, Lester Showalter. Conservative Mennonite Conference: Walter Beachy, David I. Miller, Elmer Yoder, and Leroy Yoder. Other Groups: Eric Kouns, Moses Stoltzfus, Martha (Mrs. Wayne) Weaver, Allen J. Yoder. About twenty other people were contacted by phone to determine relationships among conservative Mennonites.

Special thanks to the staff of the Lancaster Mennonite Historical Society for their valuable help in providing printed material.

CREDITS

Cover Photos: Photo of Stauffer Mennonite buggies, David Lauver; Photo of Conservative Mennontie women, Kevin and Bethany Shank; Daniel Price, 3, 55, 56, 61; Dawn Ranck, 4; Kenny Pellman, 46 bottom, 49 top, 82, 97, 157, 229; Harold Thut, 8; Good Books, 12; Archives of the Mennonite Church, (Indiana Michigan Conference Collection), left 15, (John F. Funk Collection), right 15, (D. A. Yoder Collection) top 140, (Charles Shank Collection) bottom 140, (Daniel Kauffman Collection) 141, (Paul Bender Collection) 147, (Ruth B. Stoltzfus) 149, (Mennonite Board of Missions Collection) 152, (Mennonite General Conference Photograph Collection) 153; J D. Stahl, 17, 39; David L. Hunsberger, 19, 32, 40, 46 top, 47, 58 top and bottom, 66 middle; Lancaster Mennonite Historical Society, 21, 112, 145; Jerry Irwin, 26, 35, 36 bottom, 49 bottom, 62; Mel Horst, 29, 36 top, 45, 71, 88, 106; Steve Scott, 31, 65 top and bottom, 66 top and bottom, 74, 76 top and bottom, 77, 80, 81, 83, 85, 94 top, 109, 111, 113, 116, 124, 130, 132 top and bottom, 165, 170, 174, 176, 181, 202 top and bottom, 203, 206, 216, 231; Kevin and Bethany Shank, 34 top and bottom, 64, 183, 205, 211 all, 217, 220, 221, 224, 226 top and bottom; Jeff Sprang, 42 top and bottom, 43, 51 bottom; Peter Zimberg, 48, 50 top, 51 top; David Lauver, 60 top, 90, 91, 94 bottom, 95, 96, 98, 99, 100; Beth Oberholtzer, 50 bottom, 60 bottom, 78; Richard Reinhold, 86; UPI/Corbis-Bettman, 118; Harold E. Huber, 122; Willard Mayer, 128-129, LaMar Weaver, Rosedale Mennonite Missions, 131, 133, 134, 135; Mennonite Historians of Eastern Pennsylvania, 138, 144; Menno Simons Historical Library, Eastern Mennonite University, 142, 146, The Sword and Trumpet, 150; Mennonite Media Ministries, 154; Life Lines of the Southeastern Mennonite Conference, 160, 161; James Landis, 168-169; Craig Heisey, 185, 204; Logos used with permission of individual organizations, 200; Messiah Bible School, 207 all; Heritage Bible School, 208 all; Rod and Staff Publishers, 213 all, 230; Northern Youth Programs, 216 top. Illustration on page 23 copied from the Church and Sunday School House with Supplement, copyright 1902, renewal 1930 by the Mennonite Publishing House, Scottdale, Pa. 15683, used with permission.

Design by Dawn J. Ranck

Library of Congress Cataloging-in-Publication Data

Scott, Stephen, 1948-
    An introduction to Old Order and Conservative Mennonite groups / Stephen E. Scott.
    p. cm.
    Includes bibliographical references and index.
    ISBN 1-56148-101-7 (pbk.)
    1. Old Order Mennonites. 2. Conservative Mennonite Conference. 3. Mennonites.
I. Title.
BX8129.043S35   1996
289-7'3--dc20   96-22482
                                                               CIP

Table of Contents

An Introduction
to the Mennonites

The name Mennonite often evokes an image of somberly dressed rural folks who travel about with horses and buggies and refuse to take part in the military. In reality most Mennonites dress in fashionable clothing, drive modern cars, and live very much like their neighbors in urban and suburban North America. However, many of these modern Mennonites still practice non-resistance or pacifism, refusing to participate in any form of violence.

These folks sometimes do not appreciate the austere perception many people have of them. They are occasionally quick to explain that it is the Amish who actually live the kind of separated life frequently associated with the Mennonites.

However, there are also thousands of Mennonites who have no Amish connections who dress in a distinctive garb, drive horse drawn vehicles, and live separately from the mainstream of secular

The popular image of Mennonites is of plainly dressed rural folks who live simple lives. That is true of the Old Order Mennonites shown above.

Many North American Mennonites have blended quite thoroughly into the larger society, as this crowd photo taken at the 1990 Mennonite World Conference in Winnipeg, Manitoba, demonstrates.

and religious society. These are the Old Order Mennonites.

Many thousand additional Mennonites have been more open to modern technology and church programs but like the Old Order Mennonites have been quite firm in preserving a separated lifestyle, including modest, plain dress. These are the conservative Mennonites.

The Old Order and conservative Mennonites stem from the largest group of Mennonites in North America, officially known as the Mennonite Church (note the capital C for Church). This group has also been called the (Old) Mennonite Church (note the parentheses around Old) to distinguish them from other groups of Mennonites. It is important not to confuse (Old) Mennonites with Old Order Mennonites. The designation "Old" signifies that they are descended from the "original" body of Mennonites, which had its beginnings in 16th century Europe.

Mennonite Beginnings

The Mennonite Church descends from the Swiss branch of Mennonites founded in Zurich, Switzerland, in 1525. At first Mennonites were called Anabaptists because they rebaptized those who had been christened as infants. They believed baptism should be a voluntary act of an adult believer. This was one of the main points of contention between the emerging Protestant movement and the group which came to be called Anabaptists. The Anabaptist-Mennonites also believed, in contrast to the Catholics and Protestants, that the church should be composed only of truly converted Christians living dedicated, holy lives. They were convinced there should be complete separation of church and state and that followers of Christ could take no part in any form of violence, including self-defense.

A separate movement of Anabaptists developed in Holland and produced a leader named Menno Simons. Both the Dutch and Swiss Anabaptists eventually took their name—Mennonite—from him. In Switzerland, Holland, and what is now Germany the Anabaptist-Mennonites experienced severe persecution from both Catholics and Protestants. Thousands of Mennonites were exiled, imprisoned, tortured, and martyred for their faith. Persecution in Switzerland was especially long lasting and severe. Many Swiss Mennonites found a small degree of tolerance in the German Palatinate, beginning in the 1670s. However, even in the Palatinate it was small, and they were put under many restrictions and limitations. (For example, they could not own land.)

To America

When William Penn opened a haven of religious freedom in North America, these persecuted peoples were among the first to take him up on his offer. Mennonites of Dutch background from Krefeld, Germany, were aboard the *Concord* which brought the first Germanic settlers to the New World in 1683. A trickle of Dutch-related Mennonites continued migrating to Pennsylvania into the first years of the 18th century.

Then in 1707 a much larger migration of Swiss-related Mennonites from the Palatinate began. These people first settled in the area north of Philadelphia in Montgomery and Bucks Counties. The churches they established developed into the Franconia Mennonite Conference. In 1710 the first Mennonite settlers arrived in Lancaster County, Pennsylvania, which would eventually become the largest Mennonite settlement in the world. Two of the heaviest concentrations of Mennonites in Lancaster County were at Groffdale

Mennonites get their name from Menno Simons (1496-1561), a Dutch Anabaptist leader.

(started by Hans Graeff in 1717) and Weaverland (started by Henry Weber in 1721), both near present-day New Holland.

Mennonites, often coming by way of Pennsylvania, made their way into many other North American communities, establishing settlements in Virginia, Ohio, Indiana, Illinois, and Ontario by the mid 1800s.

All these scattered Mennonites churches of Swiss-Palatine background recognized each other as people of like faith but had no overall church government. Regional annual and bi-annual conferences were organized in which the ordained men met to discuss and settle church-related matters. It was not until 1898 that many of the regional conferences met in what became known as the Mennonite General Conference (not to be confused with the General Conference Mennonite Church). In 1971 this wider organization became the Mennonite Church General Assembly.

The Amish

A few years after the first Mennonites came to America, the Swiss-related Mennonites in Switzerland, Alsace, and the Palatinate became embroiled in a controversy that left the church permanently divided. Jacob Ammann, a young Mennonite bishop, began advocating a number of practices that many Swiss Mennonites could not accept. Among these were feet washing, the shunning of excommunicated members, having communion twice a year, and greater simplicity in dress.

In 1693, following a serious disagreement with the elder Swiss bishop, Hans Reist, Ammann declared himself out of fellowship with all those who would not accept his teachings. Ammann's followers became the Amish.

While the Mennonite Church is largely composed of descendents of Swiss Mennonites who remained under the leadership of Hans Reist, these Mennonites, who had separated from the Amish, adopted some characteristics typical of the Amish after coming to America. These adoptions may or may not have been due to Amish influence.

For example, feetwashing was not practiced by the early North American Mennonites, but throughout the 1800s it became more and more common. Having communion twice a year was another practice adopted by the Swiss Mennonites in America which had been an Amish distinctive in Europe. And some Mennonites in America put almost as much emphasis on simple, plain dress as the Amish.

Between 1917 and 1927 a large influx of Amish came into the Mennonite Church. These were liberal Amish, called Amish Mennonites, who had divided with the Old Order Amish in the late 1800s and organized three regional conferences. Ironically, these Amish Mennonites were generally less conservative than the (Old) Mennonites with whom they merged.

Most midwestern Mennonite churches are descended from the

The progressive Amish Mennonites to which these Wayne County, Ohio, women belonged merged with the Mennonite Church between 1917 and 1927. The movement away from distinctive plain dress is clearly illustrated in this 1908 four-generation photograph.

Amish Mennonites. Very few churches or individuals that descend from these Amish Mennonites contributed to the post-1950 conservative Mennonite movement, the group which is one of the two main focuses of this book.

Another group of Amish Mennonites, however, did play an influential part in the conservative Mennonite movement. These were independent Amish Mennonite churches who never affiliated with the three conferences that eventually merged with the Mennonite Church. These churches were more conservative than the majority of Amish Mennonites but not as traditional as the Old Order Amish. They eventually organized the Conservative Amish Mennonite Conference and the Ontario Amish Mennonite Conference. Both these groups gradually lost most of their Amish distinctives and, dropping the word Amish from their names, became the Conservative Mennonite Conference and the Western Ontario Mennonite Conference.

Another group, the Beachy Amish Mennonites, developed from the Old Order Amish beginning in the early 1900s. These people are

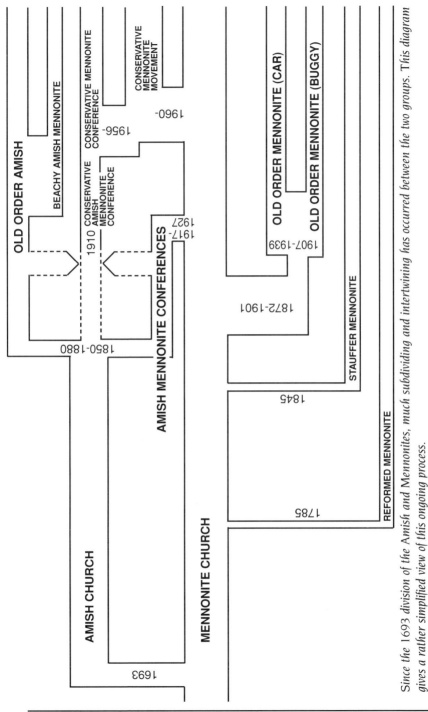

Since the 1693 division of the Amish and Mennonites, much subdividing and intertwining has occurred between the two groups. This diagram gives a rather simplified view of this ongoing process.

very similar to many conservative Mennonites and often work closely with them.

While most of today's Old Order and conservative Mennonites are descended from Swiss-Palatine Mennonite groups, they have also been heavily influenced by various Amish groups through the years.

Russian Mennonites

It has already been said that there were two separate streams in the European Anabaptist movement—the Swiss and the Dutch. While a few Dutch Mennonites were among the first settlers of Pennsylvania, it was two centuries later (the 1870s) before significant numbers of Mennonites of Dutch background came to America. These were descendents of the Dutch Mennonites who had settled in the area around Danzig (now Gdansk, Poland) in the 16th century, moved on to Ukraine in the late 1700s and early 1800s, and later to other parts of the Russian Empire. They have usually been called Russian Mennonites.

After they were established in the United States and Canada, the great majority of Russian Mennonites either incorporated into the General Conference Mennonite Church or were affiliated with the Mennonite Brethren Church.

A number of smaller, conservative groups also developed among the North American Russian Mennonites. The story of those conservative Mennonite groups belongs to a different chapter in the broader Mennonite story.

This book focuses on the Old Order Mennonite movement of the late 19th and early 20th centuries and on the mid-20th century conservative Mennonite movement.

The Old Order Mennonites

1.
The Beginnings
of the
Old Order Mennonite Movement

For more than 150 years after becoming established in North America, the doctrines and practices of people in the main body of the Swiss-Palatine Mennonite Church were relatively stable. These descendents of the Anabaptists gathered in plain meetinghouses to sing praises in their beloved German language and hear the Word

Some of the first Mennonites to settle in Lancaster County, Pennsylvania, worshiped in this house built by Christian Herr in 1719.

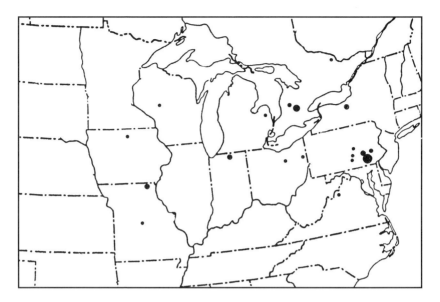

○ *Mennonite Church Communities 1870-1900*
● *Communities where Old Order groups formed*

of God proclaimed in the same tongue. The worship was pure and simple, no frills, no excitement. The ministry was chosen by lot from the congregation and received no formal training and no salary. The Sunday morning service was considered sufficient to meet the congregation's spiritual needs. Mennonites saw the spiritual nurture of their children and letting their "light so shine among men" as their main responsibilities as Christians. There was little knowledge of the needs of the physically and spiritually destitute beyond their rural communities.

At first, Mennonites resisted the stirrings in the religious world around them. Then the Methodist-inspired revival movement swept through the Pennsylvania German population in the late 1700s, attracting many Mennonites. By the mid 1800s, scattered upsurges of revivalism and progressivism had created significant movements, many of which became alienated from the main body of Mennonites. By the last third of the 19th century, most Mennonites were ready for change. They were no longer content with the time-honored ways of their ancestors. Two men were primarily responsible for leading most of the Mennonite Church into the modern world.

The Instigators of Change

In 1858, a twenty-three-year-old lad of Mennonite background far from his Bucks County, Pennsylvania, home responded to the invitation given at a Presbyterian revival meeting in Chicago. The youth was John Fretz Funk and this simple event began a course of inalterable change in the Mennonite Church. Funk's conversion brought him into the exciting world of American revivalism, and he would ultimately be instrumental in leading most of the Mennonite Church into this new realm.

While John Funk was enamored by the vitality of Evangelicalism, he did not wish to abandon his own ancestral faith. In 1859, Funk returned briefly to Pennsylvania where he was baptized into the Mennonite Church. Funk deeply appreciated the Mennonite Church but felt that much could be gained by adopting the aggressive methods of evangelical Protestantism. He was especially impressed by Sunday schools and pushed for their adoption. Funk also saw the need for Christian literature among Mennonites. In 1864, John Funk began publishing The Herald of Truth and the companion German publication, Herold der Wahrheit. These were the first successful periodicals issued by Mennonites and were widely received across the country. Although Funk used much material written by Mennonites, he also published a large percentage of writings from evangelical Protestants. Funk's publications succeeded in planting popular American Protestant ideas throughout the Mennonite Church.

John F. Funk was ordained as a Mennonite minister in 1865, widening his sphere of influence. In 1867, Funk sold the lumber business that had taken him to Chicago and moved to the growing Mennonite community in Elkhart County, Indiana, where he continued his publishing endeavors. He also traveled widely among Mennonite communities and helped to conduct the first series of "protracted" meetings—as revival meetings were then called—in the Mennonite Church at Masontown, Pennsylvania, in 1872.

In 1879, John F. Funk invited a promising young Mennonite preacher from Virginia, John S. Coffman, to join his work. Coffman became assistant editor of the Herald of Truth and produced much Sunday school literature. However, Coffman's evangelistic activity was probably even more effective than his literary work.

Coffman conducted his first series of revival meetings in Michigan in 1881 and had hundreds of such speaking engagements over the

John F. Funk (left) and John S. Coffman (right) were prime instigators in bringing revivalism and evangelical Protestant practices into the Mennonite Church in the late 1800s.

next several years. He had a deep concern for Mennonite youth and was distressed by the loss of a large percentage of them. He saw the need to use new measures to keep the wandering sheep in the fold. John S. Coffman also promoted Sunday school conferences, Bible conferences, and mission activity. He was instrumental in starting the Elkhart Institute in 1894, the first (Old) Mennonite institution of higher learning which later became Goshen College. Coffman's intensely active career in the Mennonite Church was cut short by his untimely death at age 50 in 1899.

The radical changes that John F. Funk and John S. Coffman helped bring about in the Mennonite Church during the last third of the 19th century have been viewed by some historians as a "great awakening." Funk and Coffman are looked upon as heroes of the faith who rescued the church from oblivion. Some recent historians not wishing to infer that the era before Funk and Coffman was one of spiritual deadness and lethargy have more charitably referred to this period as a time of "quickening."[1] To be sure the late 1800s saw sweeping changes in the Mennonite Church, forever transforming its emphasis and image.

While most Mennonites welcomed the innovations in the church, some were cautious and even opposed to change. Those who were cautious saw the new programs and institutions as contrary to the spirit of traditional Mennonite beliefs. They questioned following trends and techniques originating from popular modern churches who had no convictions on the cherished doctrines of non-resistance and non-conformity. They saw the introduction of Sunday schools, revival meetings, colleges, organized missions, and English church services as an open door to pull the Mennonite Church into the worldliness of American Protestantism. Several Mennonite leaders at different times and different places tried to shut the door to modernity or at least keep their flocks from going through it. These scattered islands of conservatism eventually formed a loose fellowship known as Old Order Mennonites. The story of their struggle against the forces of change follows.

Indiana

People from many different Mennonite communities were drawn to the flat and fertile land of northern Indiana in the 1840s. One of these was Jacob Wisler who moved from Columbiana County, Ohio, to Elkhart County, Indiana, in 1848. Wisler was ordained a preacher in Ohio and was advanced to the position of bishop in Indiana in 1851. Wisler's staunch conservatism clashed with two very progressive Mennonite preachers who moved into the same area in the 1860s—Daniel Brenneman and John F. Funk.

These and other progressives chafing under Wisler's conservatism, sought to have Wisler silenced. They were ultimately successful. Jacob Wisler's ministry was suspended for the first time in 1867 (the year Funk moved to the area), and after repeated attempts at reconciliation, he was expelled from the Indiana Mennonite Conference on January 6, 1872, along with preachers Christian Bare and John Weaver.[2] About 100 members sided with Wisler.[3]

Wisler's group initially met for worship at the Yellow Creek, Shaum's, and Blosser meetinghouses at times when the larger groups were not using them. The Indiana Conference or "Funk" Mennonites built their own Yellow Creek meetinghouse in 1912, leaving the old meetinghouse for the Wisler Group.[4]

Jacob Wisler's primary offense was his refusal to accept the innovations that were being introduced into the Mennonite Church.

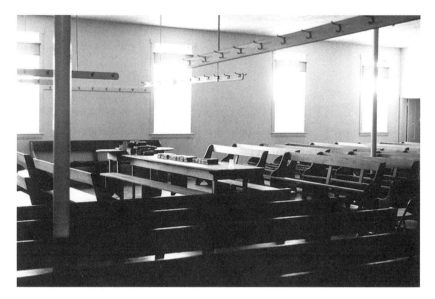

The traditional emphasis on simplicity of worship was preserved by the Old Order Mennonites as demonstrated by the austerity of the furnishings in this Groffdale Conference meetinghouse in Pennsylvania.

Wisler wanted to maintain church practices as they had been when he moved to Indiana from Ohio in 1848. The changes to which he objected included four-part singing rather than simple singing in unison, exuberant Methodist-like preaching as opposed to the usual calm steady delivery, and having an audible prayer at the beginning of the service rather than the traditional silent prayer. Wisler also did not see the introduction of evening meetings and Sunday school as necessary. Wisler's refusal to support Sunday schools after the Indiana Conference officially approved it in 1870 was the main reason given for his expulsion.

Jacob Wisler was the first Mennonite bishop to face the censure of the aggressively revivalistic element in the church, which was rapidly gaining the upper hand. Other conservatives would eventually follow Wisler's lead, but Jacob died on May 1, 1889, just before the movement he started affected some of the oldest and largest Mennonite communities in the United States and Canada. All Old Order Mennonites have sometimes been referred to as Wisler Mennonites, but currently this term has a more limited usage (see chapter 3).

Ohio

After Jacob Wisler's dismissal from the Indiana Mennonite Conference, he tried to find support at the Ohio Mennonite Conference in the spring of 1872. While the conference as a whole did not identify with Wisler's cause, a significant minority did give him a hearing. A few weeks after the Ohio Conference, Jacob Wisler and a group of ordained men organized a separate conference at the home of minister Henry Beery of the Maple Hill-Guilford Mennonite Church of Medina County, Ohio. Eight widely scattered congregations in Ohio became part of Wisler's newly formed Ohio-Indiana Mennonite Conference.

All of Bishop John Shaum's Chester Mennonite Church in the western part of Wayne County, Ohio, sided with Wisler as well as many members of the Martin's-Pleasant View church in eastern Wayne County. The majority of Bishop Abraham Rohrer's Maple Hill-Guilford congregation in Medina County and a small percentage of the Mahoning County Mennonites also affiliated with the Wisler group.[5]

Four Ohio churches which sided with Wisler eventually became extinct—those in Seneca County, Ashland County, Wood County, and Williams County.[6]

Ontario

Meanwhile, six bishops of the Ontario Mennonite Conference declared in 1871 that their churches should have no association with Jacob Wisler and his followers in Indiana.[7] Despite this decree, there was widespread support for Wisler's conservative stance among Ontario Mennonites. The innovations, such as Sunday school, revival meetings, and use of the English language, which had caused controversy in the United States were also provoking contention in Canada.

Sometime in the late 1870s, Abraham Martin, a bishop in Waterloo County, Ontario, invited a group of ordained men to his home to determine what should be their course of action. At this meeting Abraham's father, John Martin, spoke of the responsibility of parents to teach their children religious principles in the home. He suggested that if this were practiced, there would be no need for Sunday schools. The group was strongly determined to remain opposed to Sunday schools and even conceded that they would cease their opposition to evening meetings and English preaching if

The Ontario Old Order Mennonites shown here descend from those who resisted changes in forms of worship, which were being introduced into the Mennonite Church in the late 1800s.

Sunday school would be stopped.[8] In 1879, the Waterloo County Mennonite community was divided into three bishop districts with Abraham Martin in charge of the Woolwich Township District.[9] This made it possible for Martin to work somewhat independently of other Mennonites in the area.

For several weeks in 1885, Noah Stauffer and Solomon Gehman held evening meetings in the homes of several Mennonite families just north of the town of Waterloo. About 30 people experienced conversion during the course of these meetings and asked for baptism. These converts lived in Bishop Abraham Martin's Woolwich district, but Martin refused to baptize them because he questioned the validity of the revivalism through which they were converted. The 30 people went to a neighboring district and were baptized by Bishop Elias Weber at Breslau.[10]

The baptism issue generated intense debate but the Ontario Conference issued a peace resolution in 1885 and was determined not to divide the church.[11] Despite this effort, Abraham Martin with several other ordained men withdrew from the conference in 1887.

In 1888, Martin held a special conference at the Martin meeting-house north of Waterloo. The final break occurred in 1889 when two separate conferences were held after a controversy on the date of the conference.[12]

Abraham Martin's Woolwich district in Waterloo County with four meetinghouses constituted the largest Old Order following in Ontario. Nearly all the Mennonites in this district sided with the Old Order. An Old Order community also formed in the vicinity of Markham just north of Toronto, and several small Old Order churches existed at Vineland, Stevensville, Cayuga-Rainham in the Niagara peninsula, and Zurich in Huron County. The four small groups have become extinct, and the community in Markham is also nearly extinct.

Pennsylvania

The Mennonites of Lancaster County, Pennsylvania, were generally rather cautious of innovations but the changes that had started in the midwest eventually reached this largest of all Mennonite communities. English preaching came in very gradually, beginning in the 1850s. In 1871, the Lancaster Mennonite Conference agreed to permit Sunday school in districts where there was unanimous agreement for its introduction.

However, Bishop George Weaver kept a tight rein on his large Weaverland-Groffdale-Bowmansville District. He staunchly resisted the introduction of Sunday school and English church services. Jonas Martin became the senior bishop after Weaver's death in 1883 and continued in the same straight and narrow way, but with increasing difficulty. When Bishop Christian Shaum, the successor of Jacob Wisler in Indiana, visited Lancaster County in 1889, Bishop Isaac Eby (one of the first Lancaster Mennonites who preached only in English) wrote Jonas Martin a letter warning him to have no part with this man.[13] Eby accurately perceived that Martin and Shaum were of like mind and was evidently trying to prevent any encouragement of Jonas Martin's conservatism.

When a new meetinghouse was built for the Lichty's congregation in Jonas Martin's district, a new style pulpit on a raised platform was installed without approval from the district council. Traditionally, the Lancaster County Mennonites had only simple tables for the preachers which were on the same level as the congregation. This symbolized the equality of the ministry and the laity. Those who favored a pulpit at Lichty's said they wanted to make it easier for one-armed preacher John Zimmerman to handle his Bible. There were those in the congregation who felt very strongly that the changes in the meetinghouse were serious departures from time-honored practices. Some of these people secretly broke into Lichty's several evenings before the dedication service for the new building on September 26, 1889, removed the pulpit and platform, and replaced them with a traditional preacher's table.

This clandestine act incensed the progressive element in the Lancaster Conference. Jonas Martin was accused of sympathizing with the culprits and of not disciplining them. After several years of agitation about the incident, Jonas Martin was asked to make a public confession of his error and to refrain from serving communion in the spring of 1893.[14] Martin agreed to this.

Over this same time, another source of turbulence was the opening of a Sunday school at the Weaverland schoolhouse in June 1891. When the crowd could not be accommodated in the school, the

A point of controversy among the late 19th century Lancaster Conference Mennonites involved the use of pulpits. Here we see an early form of the pulpit on a raised platform at the Weaverland Mennonite Church near New Holland, Pennsylvania. The old preachers' table is still present immediately in front of the pulpit in this 1920s photograph.

The transition from German to English and from traditional to revivalistic forms of worship is demonstrated in this comparison of hymn books. The German hymnal (above) was first published by the Lancaster Mennonite Conference in 1804 and is still used today by the Old Order Mennonites. The Church and Sunday School Hymnal (facing page) first appeared among Mennonites in 1902 and reflects the acceptance of fast-tempo Gospel songs.

Sunday school was moved to the Weaverland meetinghouse. Since this move was unauthorized, it soon came to the attention of the church council which voted by a large majority to close the Sunday school. Over this time of controversy, many members at Weaverland did not kneel in prayer with the congregation to demonstrate their lack of unity with the church on this issue.[15]

Two decisions of the Lancaster Mennonite Conference were especially disturbing to Jonas Martin. It had been the policy among Mennonites not to perform marriages of couples unless both were members of the Mennonite Church. Since many people of Mennonite background resorted to having ministers of other denominations perform their marriages, many in the Lancaster Conference felt it would be better to allow their own ordained men to seal the vows. When the issue was brought before the conference in 1884, it was soundly turned down. However, in 1892 that ruling was changed.

The second matter concerned the procurement of a legal charter

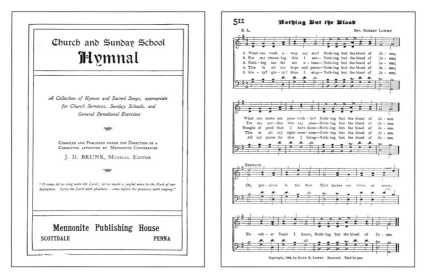

by the Kauffman Mennonite Church in order to receive property left to the church by Abraham Kauffman, a wealthy banker and politician who died in 1886. The Lancaster Conference discipline of 1881 stated that no member shall "use the government to settle an estate." Jonas Martin saw the Kauffman charter as a violation of that ruling.

On October 6, 1893, Martin stood before the fall session of the Lancaster Mennonite Conference and stated his grievances.

> I am also at one with the old ground and counsel, but not with the new things that have been introduced. Giving together into marriage such that are outside of the church and with the Sunday Schools that are not held in peace nor with those that have it thus am I not at one. If something is passed that is not good, one can change it again, one needs not to let it so. I have for a long time already agreed to these things against my conscience and I want to continue no longer in this or keep house this way.[16]

After hearing Martin, the other bishops went to another room where they concluded that Jonas had been too critical of the conference rulings. Martin was called in and asked to confess his wrongdoing. According to one report, one bishop pulled out a pocket watch and gave Martin ten minutes to recant. Jonas refused and walked out of the meeting and met with a group of sympathizers outside. The conference then took action against Martin, revoking both his ministry and membership.[17]

About a third of the Weaverland-Groffdale-Bowmansville District sided with Jonas Martin and organized the Weaverland Mennonite Conference. Of the meetinghouses in the district the "Martinites," as they came to be called, found themselves locked out of Weaverland, Groffdale, Metzlers, and Bowmansville. Martindale and Churchtown were left open on the off Sundays (congregations usually met every other Sunday at the time) for the Martin group's use.

The Martinites (Weaverland Mennonite Conference) built new meetinghouses at Weaverland in 1894, Groffdale in 1895, Pequea in 1896 (an English speaking congregation in Leacock Township), Bowmansville in 1902, and Churchtown in 1910. The Martindale meetinghouse was shared by the Lancaster Conference and the Old Order Mennonites until 1948 when the Lancaster Conference congregation built a more modern building.

Virginia

The Mennonites in the Shenandoah Valley of Virginia were impacted by outside influences at an earlier date than most other Mennonites. They were among the first Mennonites to make the transition to English and published the first widely used English Mennonite hymnal in 1847. Sunday schools were officially approved by the Virginia Mennonite Conference in 1868. Despite the general progressiveness of the Virginia Mennonites, a small conservative minority resisted change.

Foremost among these traditionalists was Abraham Blosser, who published an unabashedly conservative periodical called *The Watchful Pilgrim* from 1880 to 1888. This publication was in direct opposition to John F. Funk's *Herald of Truth* .

However, the real trouble in Virginia began in 1894 when Bishop Lewis J. Heatwole became the sole bishop of the Middle District. Heatwole had actually been ordained bishop in Missouri, where he had lived for several years. He became a senior bishop in Virginia somewhat by default after his father-in-law, Bishop Samuel Coffman, died.[18]

Bishop Heatwole was married to the sister of pioneer Mennonite evangelist, John Coffman, and he was in sympathy with his brother-in-law's progressive ideas. This tendency caused consternation among a conservative minority in the district. The first flare-up occurred on December 10, 1895, when Bishop Heatwole departed from established traditions in a pre-ordination sermon. The conservative element in the church, which included several ordained men, accumulated a number of charges against Heatwole during 1896 and 1897. Several council meetings were held to resolve the differences but to no avail.[19]

On March 20, 1898, conservative-minded minister Simeon Heatwole and two other men were put out of the church because of their refusal to abide by the counsel of the church. Simeon later announced a meeting of those who were like minded at the Bank Mennonite meetinghouse. At the appointed time, the group found themselves locked out, so they held the meeting outside.[20]

The lines, however, were not clearly drawn between the two groups until September 4, 1900,[21] when all members of the Middle District were asked to give their allegiance to the decisions of the Virginia Mennonite Conference. By March 31, 1901, seventy-one members had refused to compromise and were thus disowned.[22]

In September 1902, Bishop John Martin of the Old Order Mennonite Church in Indiana came to Virginia, held communion, and baptized fifteen youths. Two months later Bishop Jonas Martin of the Pennsylvania Old Order Mennonites conducted an ordination in Virginia in which Simeon Heatwole was made bishop and John Dan Wenger was ordained to the ministry.[23] The Virginia Old Orders were denied use of the existing Mennonite church buildings, so they constructed their own Pleasant View meetinghouse in 1902 and Oak Grove in 1923.[24]

Conservatism in Other Communities

As has been noted, Old Order groups were formed in most of the larger settlements of Mennonites in North America. Even so, a few settlements were unaffected by the divisions. No Old Order element emerged in the large Franconia Mennonite Conference just north of Philadelphia. The churches in this conference, though quite traditional in some respects, were not as conservative in many outward matters and had experienced the withdrawal of a liberal faction in 1847 under the leadership of John H. Oberholtzer (which became part of the General Conference Mennonite Church). But there was some sympathy in the Franconia Conference for the Old

Distinctive plain dress was not a major issue in the Old Order divisions of the late 1800s and the mode of transportation was not an issue at all. (Automobiles were only in the early stages of development.) The Old Order groups which formed continued to uphold conservative dress standards, but the Mennonite Church at the time also promoted non-conformity in attire. The simple, modest dress practices and horse drawn vehicles preserved by the Groffdale Conference (Wenger) Old Order Mennonites are illustrated here.

Order movement, especially from preacher Jacob Mensch who carried on correspondence with Old Order leaders on a regular basis. Mensch opposed Sunday schools and English church services and stressed great simplicity of life.

After Jonas Martin formed a separate group, Jacob Mensch wrote that he would feel more comfortable to go along with the Old Order side of the division but would be the only one in his church to do so.[25] Preacher J. Clayton Kolb had similar convictions and was silenced from the ministry in 1904 for opposing Sunday schools. Shortly after 1910 he moved to Lancaster County and joined the Old Order Mennonites.[26]

The Mennonite community in the Cumberland Valley of Franklin County, Pennsylvania, and Washington County, Maryland, also escaped having an Old Order-progressive division. The people in the Cumberland Valley were just as conservative in dress as Old Order Mennonites, but they adopted Sunday school and English church services with only a minimum of opposition.

Conclusion

As the Mennonite Church determined to go down the road of American Evangelicalism in the late 1800s, a minority of members did not view this path as part of the straight and narrow way. Most of these people were forced out of the church because they refused to sanction the innovations of the dominate group. Others left voluntarily when they deemed it futile to stand against the flow. The conservative factions that formed into separate fellowships in Indiana, Ohio, Ontario, Pennsylvania, and Virginia differed slightly in some areas of practice but recognized each other as being of the same faith. In the early part of the 20th century they came to be identified as Old Order Mennonites.

2.
Traveling Slowly in the Straight and Narrow Way: The Horse-and-Buggy Old Order Mennonites

As has been noted, the Old Order Mennonite movement developed from a series of divisions over a period of three decades (1872-1901) in four widely separated areas (Indiana-Ohio, Ontario, Pennsylvania, and Virginia). The issues mainly centered around forms of worship and church activity.

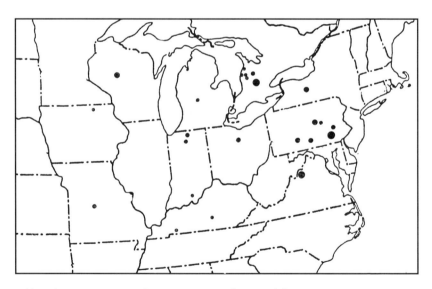

Old Order Mennonite Settlements in 1996 (horse-and-buggy groups)
(Does not include Stauffer-related groups)

When the Weaverland Old Order Mennonite Conference permitted car ownership in 1927, minister Joseph Wenger started a separate group to preserve the old ways. Here members of the Groffdale Conference group founded by Wenger are shown leaving the Martindale, Pennsylvania, meetinghouse.

Almost before the dust settled from this division, the Old Orders were faced with another set of conflicts within their own fellowships. This time the key issues related to daily living. The Old Order Mennonites had to decide how much of the rapidly advancing world of modern technology they could accept without becoming "of the world." In the course of three more decades (1907-1939), they divided among themselves into two distinct fellowships—those who allowed cars and those who did not. This chapter introduces those groups who do not drive cars—the Groffdale Conference (Wengers) of Pennsylvania, the Ohio-Indiana Conference (which merged with the Groffdale Conference in 1973), the Ontario Conference (Woolwichers), and the Virginia Conference (Russel Cline group).

The Groffdale Conference "Wenger" Mennonites

The founding bishop of the Lancaster County, Pennsylvania, Old Order Mennonites, Jonas H. Martin, died in 1925, leaving the leadership of the Weaverland Mennonite Conference in the hands of

TABLE ONE
The Horse-and-Buggy Old Order Mennonite Groups

Groffdale (Old Order) Mennonite Conference

Alternate Name: Wenger Mennonites
Numbers: 5,464 members (estimated 1992)

Settlements	Founded	Meetinghouses
Lancaster County, PA	Original	10
*Elkhart County, IN	Original	3
Berks County, PA	1949	2
Union County, PA	1960	2
Cumberland-Franklin County, PA	1967	3
Blair-Bedford County, PA	1967	3
Morgan County, MO	1970	2
Taylor County, WI	1973	3
Richland County, OH	1973	3
Yates County, NY	1974	4
Casey County, KY	1975	1
Christian County, KY	1987	1
Montcalm County, MI	1992	1**
Floyd County, IA	1992	1
Marshall County, IN	1992	1**

Ontario (Old Order) Mennonite Conference

Alternate Name: Woolwich Mennonites, Woolwichers
Numbers: 2,200 members (estimated 1993)

Settlements	Founded	Meetinghouses
Waterloo County, Ontario	Original	9
Mt. Forest, Ontario	1967	3
Teeswater, Ontario	1990	1**
Chesley, Ontario	1993	1**
Kinloss, Ontario	1994	1**
Dunnville, Ontario	1995	1**

Virginia (Old Order) Mennonite Conference

Alternate Name: Cline Group, Showalter Group
Numbers: 400 members (estimated 1990)

Settlements	Founded	Meetinghouses
Rockingham County, Virginia	Original	3
Washington County, Indiana	1995	1**

* Ohio-Indiana (Old Order) Mennonite Conference
(Merged with Groffdale |Old Order| Mennonite Conference in 1973)
** Worship in private homes

The Yellow Creek meetinghouse in Elkhart County, Indiana, is used by the oldest group of Old Order Mennonites, founded in 1872.

Bishop Moses G. Horning (1871-1955), who had been ordained to assist Martin in 1914. Bishop Martin had made automobile ownership a test of membership, excommunicating anyone who purchased one.[1]

After Martin's death, Bishop Horning began allowing members to own cars. In 1927, a conservative faction, consisting of about half the members of the Weaverland Conference, withdrew from the Weaverland Conference under the leadership of preacher Joseph O. Wenger (1868-1956) because they opposed Horning's lenience on the automobile issue.

The newly formed group became known as the Groffdale Old Order Mennonite Conference, the main body of horse-and-buggy Mennonites in Lancaster County. Later that same year, Wenger was ordained bishop by John W. Martin of Indiana, John Dan Wenger of Virginia, and Daniel Brubacker of Michigan.[2]

In spite of their differences over the automobile question, both the Groffdale and Weaverland conference groups consider themselves Old Order Mennonite. Today, five of the meetinghouses that existed in 1927 when the Groffdale Conference withdrew from the

The large Old Order Mennonite community in Ontario is located primarily in Waterloo County. The majority of its members use horse drawn vehicles without tops.

Weaverland Conference (Horning) Mennonites are shared by both groups. One Sunday the horses and buggies of the Groffdale Conference line the church lot at a given meetinghouse, and on the next Sunday an assemblage of Weaverland Conference black cars gather at the same place. (They each worship every other week.)

The Ohio-Indiana (Old Order) Conference

Bishop John W. Martin (1852-1940) of the Indiana Old Orders opposed the introduction of telephones in the homes of members, and the use of the English language in church services during the early 1900s. In 1907 most of the ministry, but only a minority of the laity, in the Ohio-Indiana Old Order Mennonite Conference withdrew and formed a separate group under John W. Martin's leadership. Automobiles were not common enough to be an issue at the time, but they were later forbidden. Most Old Orders in Indiana and Ohio did allow cars, telephones, and the English language.

While three tiny congregations of John W. Martin's followers existed tenuously in Ohio for half a century, they were all extinct by 1970.

The small Old Order church at Emmet County, Michigan, also identified with John W. Martin, but gradually dwindled to nothing after the last minister moved away in 1939.[3]

After decades of barely holding their own, the Indiana horse-and-buggy Old Orders turned to the Groffdale Old Order Mennonite Conference of Lancaster County for support in 1973.

The Ontario Conference "Woolwich" Mennonites

The majority of the Old Order Mennonites in Ontario remained with the conservative, horse-and-buggy part of the movement and have often been called "Woolwichers" because Woolwich Township in Waterloo County was their point of origin.

In 1939, those Woolwich Old Orders who wished to have cars and more modern conveniences formed the Markham-Waterloo Conference. Three of the original Old Order meetinghouses in Ontario were shared by the Woolwich and the Markham-Waterloo groups in the same manner as the Wenger and Horning Mennonites in Pennsylvania. The Martin meetinghouse, on the edge of the growing city of Waterloo, was completely given over to the Markham-Waterloo Conference in 1993 because of the increasing difficulty for horse-drawn travel in this urbanized area. The Woolwich group may still conduct funerals and have burials in the cemetery at the Martin meetinghouse.

The Virginia Conference "Cline" Mennonites

The main group of Old Order Mennonites in Virginia has experienced steady growth since its beginnings in 1901, despite schisms and losses to more modern groups.

While there was no large scale car-buggy division in Virginia, a major division occurred in 1953, primarily because of personality differences between Bishop John Dan Wenger and Preacher Russel Cline.[4] The Pennsylvania Groffdale Conference gave assistance to the Cline group, but the group did not join the Groffdale Conference. The Cline group organized separately as the Virginia Old Order Mennonite Conference.

Both the Russel Cline and the John Dan Wenger groups drive horses and buggies and do not allow automobiles. They do continue to share some meetinghouses, but do not fellowship with each other.

Two groups of horse-and-buggy Old Order Mennonites meet on alternate Sundays at two meetinghouses in Rockingham County, Virginia. Two Old Order Mennonite buggies (top) travel a back road in Rockingham County. Old Order Mennonites gather for worship (bottom) in Virginia.

The Wider Old Order Mennonite Fellowship

While these regional Old Order Mennonite conferences have worked together in many church matters, they each also remain autonomous groups. In basic standards all are in general agreement, but the differences in rules relating to technology put some limitations on inter-fellowship. There are also numerous differences in matters of practice and custom, making each regional group unique.

Education in Each of the Four Major Groups

Before the 1950s Old Order Mennonite children attended eight grades in rural one-room public schools. Further education was considered unnecessary if not harmful. The consolidation of rural schools prompted the Old Order Mennonites in Lancaster County to start their first parochial school in 1952. Five more schools were started by the end of the decade and 23 followed in the 1960s. By 1993 there were 53 Old Order Mennonite schools in Lancaster County.[5]

The Lancaster County Old Order Mennonites originally cooperated with the Old Order Amish in establishing parochial schools. While a separate Old Order Mennonite school committee was orga-

This parochial school in Lancaster County, Pennsylvania, has Groffdale Conference Old Order Mennonite, Stauffer Mennonite, and Old Order Amish students, as evidenced by the various styles of clothing.

nized in 1967, they continue to work closely with the Amish. Many of their schools are supported by families from different Old Order groups—Wenger, Horning, Stauffer, and Reidenbach Mennonites, as well as the Amish.

In Woolwich Township, Waterloo County, Ontario, the consolidation of public schools did not begin until 1965. Concerned Old Order Mennonites from both the Woolwich and Markham-Waterloo groups cooperated in establishing seven of their own parochial schools in

Old Order Mennonites believe their basic educational needs can be met by eight grades provided in one-room schools such as these in Lancaster County, Pennsylvania.

the fall of 1966.[6] Currently (1994) there are 26 Old Order Mennonite schools in the Waterloo County community with an additional seven in Wellington County (Mt. Forest).[7]

The impetus for parochial schools in the Virginia Old Order Mennonite community came when the local public school superintendent would not grant exemption for fourteen-year-olds to leave school. The matter was taken to the Virginia state legislature which transferred the responsibility of granting exemptions from the local school board to the state. The largest group of Virginia Old Order Mennonites organized their first parochial school in 1969 with two more following in the 1970s.

Many Old Order Mennonites in Indiana supported a school organized in the late 1960s in cooperation with several different plain groups. In 1978 the Indiana Old Orders started a school of their own. They now (1994) have five schools.[8]

Leadership Styles among the Old Order Mennonites

Each Old Order Mennonite congregation normally has one preacher and one deacon, chosen by lot from among the men of the congregation. All the ordained men constitute the governing body of the church which meets in conference in the spring and fall. No other representatives from the congregations or church districts attend these conferences. The ordained men of each congregation all participate in carrying out disciplinary measures and visiting the sick. Bishops are chosen from among the preachers.

Each bishop oversees several churches in a district and is responsible to perform baptisms and officiate at baptismal instruction classes, communion, ordinations, weddings, and funerals, as well as taking part in preaching and giving testimony at regular church services. He also is largely responsible for enforcing the discipline of the church, including pronouncing excommunications and receiving back into the church those who wish to restore their membership.

The main responsibility of the preacher is to preach. He also gives testimony at church services and takes part in the instruction classes. A preacher may conduct weddings and funerals in the absence of a bishop or by special invitation.

A deacon may preach on rare occasions when no preacher or bishop is present but normally only reads aloud from the Bible and gives testimony at a church service. The deacon assists the bishop

TABLE TWO

Order of Worship in Old Order Mennonite Groups

Ontario Old Order Mennonite	Groffdale Conference (Wenger Mennonite)	Virginia Old Order Mennonite
1. Ministers enter	1. Opening hymn	1. Ministers enter
2. Opening hymn	2. Ministers enter	2. Two hymns
3. Deacon reads scripture	3. Second hymn (lined by minister)	3. Opening sermon
4. Opening sermon	4. Opening sermon	4. Silent prayer
5. Silent prayer	5. Silent prayer	5. Deacon reads scripture
6. Main sermon	6. Deacon reads scripture	6. Main sermon
7. Comments from other ministers (while seated)	7. Main sermon	7. Concluding comments from other minister (standing)
8. Main speaker responds	8. Comments from other ministers (while seated)	8. Audible prayer
9. Audible prayer	9. Main speaker responds	9. Closing hymn
10. Closing hymn	10. Audible prayer	10. Announcements
11. Benediction (while seated)	11. Benediction (standing)	11. Benediction (standing)
12. Announcements	12. Closing hymn (lined by minister)	
	13. Announcements	

The traditional preachers' table with adjoining singers' table is found in all Pennsylvania Old Order Mennonite meetinghouses.

in the baptismal and communion services and provides the bread and wine for communion. Much of the work of the deacon is behind the scenes. Deacons are usually the first of the ordained to confront those who violate church rules. The financial aspects of the church, including the collection and distribution of money for the needy, are the responsibility of the deacon.

The request to ordain a deacon, minister, or bishop is brought before the members at the spring or fall congregational council meeting. If the vote is affirmative, the request is carried to the church-wide conference for the approval of the ministerial body. Later at a specified Sunday morning church service, all members are given the opportunity to go to the ordained men, usually including a bishop, seated in the ministers' council room and voice their vote

The Old Order Mennonites of Ontario make use of very simple pulpits in their austerely plain meetinghouses. The pulpit style used here traces back to Franconia Conference Mennonites in eastern Pennsylvania. Mennonites from this part of Pennsylvania were among the early Mennonite settlers in Ontario.

for the man they feel is most qualified for the church office. Normally only a few older people take this privilege except in the newer communities where younger people take part. Women are permitted to cast their votes but few actually do. All those who receive one or more votes are said to be in the ordination "class." Usually, about five to ten men receive votes. The chosen men and their wives meet with the ministerial body the following day (Monday) to have the duties and responsibilities of the given office explained. Anyone wishing to drop out may do so at this time.

The next day (Tuesday) the ordination service is held in the meetinghouse, usually with a large crowd in attendance. The men in the ordination class sit in the order of their age in the front row opposite their wives. Following sermons by a preacher and bishop, two deacons take the same number of identical hymn books as there are members in the ordination class and go to the council room. A slip of paper containing the words "The lot is cast into the lap, but the decision is wholly from the Lord" is placed in one of the books. The books are shuffled by one deacon while the other turns his back. Then the second deacon shuffles the books while the first turns his back. Then the books are brought back to the meeting room and placed on the singers' table (in the Groffdale Conference churches) or on the pulpit (in other conferences).

The congregation kneels for prayer led by the bishop. After the bishop rearranges the books, each of the men in the order they are sitting rises, takes a book, and returns to his seat. When all have chosen, the bishop in charge goes down the line and examines each book to see if it contains the lot. The man who has the book containing the lot is immediately given the ordination charge as the bishop places his hands on his head. The bishop greets him with a holy kiss.

All church offices are lifetime positions. An ordained man continues his responsibilities as long as he is able. When the infirmities of age prevent a man from fulfilling his duties, he will be given a lighter load of preaching and other church work.

Language among the Old Orders

Most Old Order Mennonites who use horse drawn transportation speak Pennsylvania German in the home, preach in a mixture of Pennsylvania German and High German, and use the Martin Luther translation of the Bible along with German hymnbooks. Occasionally, especially at funerals, some English will be used in a sermon when visitors who do not understand German are present.

English is the language of instruction in all Old Order Mennonite schools, but there are special classes to learn High German. Pennsylvania German is seldom written.

Since the transition to English had already been made well before the Old Order division in 1901, today's Virginia Old Order Mennonites are generally not bilingual. Only a few Virginia Old Orders are able to speak Pennsylvania German and an even smaller number can read High German. All Virginia Old Order church services are conducted in English. Although it might be difficult for them, visiting ministers from other communities preach in English when they come to Virginia.

Meetinghouse Styles

Old Order Mennonite meetinghouses are plain, white, rectangular, one-story structures with gable roofs. There are several

Since the 1960s, Old Order Mennonites have started many new settlements, often far from their original communities. Here a meetinghouse is being constructed near Shiloh, Ohio, by a group of people who migrated to the area from Lancaster County, Pennsylvania.

entrances around the building, each used by a different age-gender group (older men, younger men, etc.).

The interiors of the meetinghouses are starkly plain; white walls with no decoration of any kind, unvarnished floors, and simple benches with narrow backs.

In the Groffdale Conference churches the ministry sits along one of the long sides of the building on the same level as the rest of the congregation. There is no pulpit, or elevated platform, just a simple table. This arrangement is said to symbolize that the ministry is not a special class above the laity.

Old Order Mennonites in Ontario, Indiana, and Virginia all use a simple kind of wide pulpit. This feature is thought to have originated in the Franconia Mennonite Conference of Montgomery and Bucks Counties, Pennsylvania. Many of the original Mennonite settlers (forebears of the Old Order Mennonites) of Ontario, Indiana, and Virginia came from those counties in Pennsylvania and may date their heritage even further to the Dutch Mennonites who first settled this area north of Philadelphia. Even though the Lancaster and Franconia Conference Mennonites have lived in close proximity to each other, there have always been many differences in practice between the two areas.

In Ontario the floors of the meetinghouses are elevated progressively away from the preachers so as to give the people in the back rows an unobstructed view. In Virginia the preachers are positioned at one of the gable ends rather than on a side wall. There is a low platform for the pulpit. Two small sections of benches on either side of the pulpit are at right angles to the benches in the main part of the meetinghouse. These are the so-called "amen corners" reserved for older people. In all Old Order Mennonite meetinghouses males and females sit separately. There are also different sections for age groups.

On one of the gable ends of each meetinghouse are cloak rooms for the women and a minister's council room. One part of the women's cloak room serves as a nursery. There may or may not be a separate cloak room for men. The Groffdale (except Indiana) and Ontario Conference churches feature hat racks suspended from the ceiling in the men's section.

At Groffdale Conference churches, long open-sided sheds are provided for some of the horses and buggies to park during the church service. There are also many rows of hitching rails in the church yard. In Ontario and Virginia all the horses are tied at open-air hitching rails. Since there is no plumbing inside the church building there are hand water pumps and outhouses outside.

Dress

Old Order Mennonites observe definite standards of dress based on the scriptural principles of simplicity, modesty, and non-conformity. Each community or group has its own distinctive customs and practices relating to dress. The following series of pictures will illustrate these.

To attend church, Old Order Mennonite women wear black bonnets over white net head coverings. Long, simply made dresses may or may not have a cape and apron, depending on the age of the person. Black shoes and stockings are the rule. This particular scene is of Wenger Mennonites at the Weaverland Old Order Mennonite Church near New Holland, Pennsylvania.

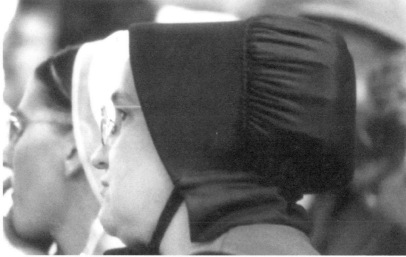

Women's bonnets vary somewhat from one community of Old Order Mennonites to the next. The styles also vary within communities, depending on the occasion and age group. In the top photo, three different types of Ontario Old Order Mennonite bonnets are seen. A regular woman's summer bonnet on the left, a girl's sunbonnet in the middle, and a "Queen Victoria" bonnet on the right (worn in the winter by women in the Ontario Old Order Mennonite Conference but year round by members of the David Martin Group). The bottom picture shows a Groffdale Conference (Wenger) Old Order Mennonite woman's bonnet.

Fabric in floral prints is perfectly acceptable to nearly all Old Order Mennonites. The braids of this girl from Ontario are typical of most Old Order Mennonite girls before the mid-teens.

Shawls rather than coats are considered more conservative by Old Order Mennonites. Shawls are worn especially for church going as is the case with these women from Ontario.

Customs regarding the wearing of head coverings differ somewhat among the various Old Order Mennonite communities. Groffdale Conference (Wenger) Mennonite girls wear coverings only to church from age two to sixteen. From age sixteen on, they wear coverings all the time. White tie strings are worn until after marriage at which time black strings are worn.

The Wenger Mennonite girls in this photo are wearing colorful sunbonnets, half of which have brims made of straw.

A plain black hat, a frock coat with standing collar, and/or a plain vest are standard apparel for mature Old Order Mennonite men. Beards are not traditional among these people. The man in the top photo is from Waterloo County, Ontario. The bottom photo is a scene from the Groffdale Conference (Wenger) Mennonites of Lancaster County, Pennsylvania.

Ontario Old Order Mennonite young men wear conventional dark suits with long neckties. Old-fashioned caps are also the rule. Young men in most other Old Order Mennonite communities wear conventional suits, but do not wear neckties. In other communities, the young men usually wear narrow brimmed alpine-style hats.

Everyday summer wear for Old Order Mennonite men and boys includes a buttoned shirt of printed fabric, suspenders, a straw hat, and blue jeans. These boys are from a Groffdale Conference settlement in Ohio.

Young People's Activities and Courtship

Groffdale Conference Mennonite young people begin attending Saturday night social activities at about age seventeen. These events take place in the homes of the youth where other family members participate in the first part of the evening activities. For about two hours there is an informal time of singing English songs. One German song is sometimes sung. The last several hours of the gathering are devoted to various kinds of games some of which resemble square dancing. (The adults and younger children in the family retire for the night before this takes place.)

During the summer, singing schools are held on Saturday evenings in several Old Order Mennonite schools in Lancaster County. In the past, these gatherings were somewhat controversial and were conducted by members of other Mennonite groups. Now Old Order members teach youth to read music and sing four-part harmony from the *Church and Sunday School Hymnal* and other more modern songbooks.

Sunday evening is the customary time for dating. A young man calls at the home of his girlfriend where the two spend a quiet evening in the parlor conversing, playing table games, and possibly singing. The old practice of bundling is strictly forbidden. In former years there was little or no interaction with other members of the girl's family, but since the 1980s, courtship has been less secretive. The date may be disturbed by roving bands of "scouters," consisting of teenage boys who have not yet found a girlfriend.

Woolwich and Indiana Old Order Mennonites have youth singings on Sunday evenings. Dating occurs after the singing.

Weddings

Old Order Mennonite weddings are traditionally held in the home of the bride, not in a church building. Between 150 and 200 people typically attend. Among the Groffdale Conference Mennonites, weddings are normally only held on Tuesdays and Thursdays. Traditionally, weddings took place in November and December. Today other times of the year, with the exception of summer, are common for weddings. A few weeks before the wedding the intentions of the couple are "published" at the end of a Sunday morning service. There is no engagement announcement before this time. Instead of an engagement ring, a young man usually gives his fiancée a special clock as a token of their relationship.

The bride traditionally wears a light gray dress with a cape and apron in the same pattern and length as her regular church-going dress. In Indiana blue is most common for wedding dresses but gray is also seen. The groom wears a black suit in the plain pattern for the first time. Before the service begins, the bride and groom wait in an upstairs room with their attendants.

The guests who are dating couples come upstairs and present their gifts and divide into separate rooms for boys and girls. Guests are served cookies and small glasses of wine before the service begins. This is said to be in observance of the biblical wedding at Cana in which Christ turned water into wine. An announcer calls out the names of the dating couples who come downstairs and are seated in a separate room from the married couples.

When everyone has been seated, the ministers and the parents of the bride go upstairs and have a brief counseling session with the bride and groom. The ministers and parents go downstairs and take their seats. The bride and groom make their entrance during the singing of the second stanza of the only hymn sung during the wedding service. It speaks of calling the bride and groom to come forth.

The actual wedding service begins about nine o'clock in the morning and consists of about two hours of preaching, ending with a simple marriage ceremony in which the bishop asks the couple several questions then pronounces a blessing on them. Testimonies from other ordained men, a kneeling prayer, and a closing hymn conclude the ceremony.

The bride and groom and all the dating couples go upstairs again while tables are set for the wedding dinner. An announcer calls out the names of those seated at the tables. The bride and groom sit at the end of a long table. There may be as many as three shifts at the tables before all have eaten.

In the afternoon there is a time of German hymn singing followed by another snack of wine and cookies. The singing resumes with selections of English hymns. During the English singing, the older couples go home. The bride's mother serves supper after which additional young people arrive for an evening of festivities.

Ontario Woolwich Mennonites have many of the same wedding customs as the Pennsylvania Old Orders. In Ontario six to eight couples serve as attendants and are usually the only young people at the wedding. The bridal party, along with the waitresses and cooks, waits upstairs until everyone is seated. There is no counseling session with the bride and groom. Wine and cookies are served before the wedding begins, but during the afternoon singing the bride and groom serve fruit juice and candy bars to the guests. Children are given the privilege to sell small bags of oranges, popcorn, and candy to the guests. The afternoon and evening singings in Ontario are completely in English. Some Woolwich weddings are held in the afternoon with supper for all the guests in the evening. The bride and most of the female guests wear navy blue dresses. Very few grooms wear the plain coat with a standing collar. A frock-style lapel coat with a turnover collar and a black necktie are the common attire of Ontario grooms.

Old Order brides in Virginia may wear white dresses, but pastel shades are also seen. Virginia weddings include only one meal, and no wine and cookies are served before or after the service.

Religious Practices at Home

Before every meal Old Order Mennonite families pause for silent prayer. However, there are no established customs regarding family and individual devotions. Many feel that Matthew 6:6, "But thou, when thou prayest, enter into thy closet, and when thou hast shut thy door, pray to thy Father which is in secret . . ." teaches that prayer is strictly an individual matter. Private bedtime prayers are practiced by most church members. Children are taught simple poem prayers.

Individuals read the Bible independently in both German and English. Some families gather for Bible reading in the morning or evening, and in some cases parents teach their children to read from the German Bible. Bible storybooks and religious books are also read. Families occasionally kneel together for silent prayer. The Old Order Mennonites do not use prayer books as the Amish do. Some families also sing hymns together, especially on Sunday evening.

Christian Principles

Uncompromising in their adherence to the principle of non-resistance, Old Order Mennonites refuse to take part in military service or any other form of violence. The law may not be used against any-

Children are highly valued in Old Order Mennonite society.

Both parents are usually very involved in child rearing.

one. Members may not serve on a jury involved in a murder trial. The swearing of oaths is forbidden.

In the days before Old Order Mennonites established their own parochial schools, many members were more involved in local affairs and voted in political elections. This practice is very rare today, but is technically permitted if done quietly.

Old Order Mennonites apply the principle of separation from the world to many areas of life. Much of the frivolity and lust for pleasure and entertainment which obsesses American society is avoided. Television, radio, record players, and tape recorders are forbidden as is attendance at movies. Musical instruments are largely discouraged, but harmonicas are tolerated and some youth have accordions. Cameras are not owned and church members do not pose for pictures nor display pictures of people in their homes.

In recent years the growing and use of tobacco has been discouraged among Groffdale Conference Mennonites. There is very little consumption of alcoholic beverages. Small amounts of wine are served at weddings, but private and social drinking is discouraged.

Interaction with the larger society at public picnics or other celebrations is forbidden. Birthday parties and family reunions are officially discouraged since they are seen to lead to too much frivolity, but in actual practice people frequently have small birthday and family gatherings. Association with non-members constitutes an "unequal yoke with unbelievers" and is avoided by prohibiting membership in lodges and unions. Although the youth have informal baseball games, participation in baseball leagues is not allowed. The spirit of competition is also avoided by not taking part in agricultural shows and fairs. Any kind of gambling is prohibited.

No member may have a life insurance policy. Liability insurance is discouraged but not forbidden. Receiving Social Security or any other kind of government assistance is strongly discouraged. The Groffdale Conference has a hospital plan which operates with voluntary contributions from the membership. The deacons appoint men to collect money from the members for the needs of the brotherhood. The church also provides for losses due to fire or storm.

The deacon appoints three men to assess each case. Many members also give money or material goods individually to the victims of tragedies. Barn raisings are still practiced in Old Order Mennonite communities.

Barn raisings are part of the Old Order Mennonite practice of mutual aid. The event illustrated here took place in Ontario.

Excommunication

When an Old Order Mennonite member disobeys the rules and regulations of the church, he or she is questioned by the ordained men and asked not to commit the offense again. This generally suffices to correct the matter, but if there is a second transgression, the guilty party is required to make a confession of his or her wrongdoing before the assembled church.

Those unwilling to admit their sin are excommunicated. Church membership may be reinstated upon confession and repentance. Expelled members are "banned" to a certain extent but not to the degree practiced by the Old Order Amish, Stauffer Mennonites, and Reformed Mennonites. There is a definite strain on social interaction between church members and the excommunicated person, but such a person is not excluded from the family table. Also no restrictions are placed on marital relations or business dealings with church members.

Funerals

In all Old Order Mennonite communities a local mortician takes the body to a funeral home and performs embalming. Among Groffdale Conference people, the dead are placed in traditional close-fitting wooden coffins which are widest at the shoulders and taper to the head and feet. A two-part hinged lid is laid back to expose the head and shoulders for viewing.

For many years the Old Order Mennonites in Ontario have purchased from local funeral directors simple, straight-sided caskets made of pressboard and covered with black cloth. Caskets are also used in Virginia, but these are made by one of the Old Order members in natural oak, walnut, or mahogany. The body is brought home on the day before the funeral for a time of visitation.

Funerals are held in the forenoon or afternoon. They begin with a small service at the home for family members. The body is then placed in a horse drawn hearse and transported to the cemetery where the coffin is placed on trestles in an open area. All those who have come to the meetinghouse to attend the funeral, file by and view the body, men on one side, women on the other. When all have paid their respects and the family has had a bit of time around the coffin, the four pall bearers carry the coffin to the hand-dug grave and lower it with straps into a rough wooden box. One of the ministers conducts a short service at the graveside. A hymn is read or sometimes sung while the caretaker of the meetinghouse and an assistant fill in the grave with shovels.

The main funeral service then takes place in the meetinghouse and is conducted very much like a Sunday morning worship service. After dismissal the immediate family and selected others go to the home of the deceased for a light meal.

Old Order Mennonite funerals are conducted in utmost simplicity. Horse drawn hearses (top photo) carry plain coffins to the cemetery.

Among Virginia Old Order Mennonites, the body is brought into the meetinghouse during the funeral service. A viewing follows the service, immediately before burial.

Groffdale Conference Homes and Farms

Groffdale Conference Mennonites never really forbad the use of electricity or telephones in the home, but leaders have consistently counseled against them and have been required not to use them in their own homes. In the early 1990s a newly ordained man challenged the consistency of this ruling.

Because the conference did not require this family to stop using electricity and telephones, two ministers and about a dozen families in Missouri and a small number of Pennsylvania members withdrew from the conference in protest to the change in rules on this matter.

The majority of Groffdale members in the new settlements and most younger families in Lancaster County do have telephones and electricity and make use of many electric appliances including refrigerators and freezers. Some have automatic washers and a few have dryers. Microwave ovens are quite rare. Dishwashers are con-

Agriculture is the preferred occupation among Old Order Mennonites. When this pursuit has been difficult in the large, old communities, new settlements have been started in other areas. This scene shows a Groffdale Conference settlement near Liberty, Kentucky.

In contrast to the Old Order Amish (shown in the background) in Lancaster County, Pennsylvania, the Groffdale Conference Old Order Mennonites allow tractors for field work and hauling. However, all self-propelled farm equipment owned by these Mennonites must have steel wheels rather than pneumatic tires. This is an effort to prevent tractors from being used for road transportation.

sidered luxury items and are not used. Televisions, radios and other entertainment devices are taboo because of the harmful influences they bring into the home. Air conditioners are usually only used when needed for health reasons.

On the other hand, there are some Groffdale Mennonites who voluntarily do without modern technology. They do not have electricity, telephones, and central heating. A few do not have indoor bathrooms. A higher percentage of people choose this path in Lancaster County than in most of the more recent branch communities.

The great majority of Old Order Mennonites are engaged in farming. There are some small businesses and cottage industries, but an overall devotion to the agricultural life is supported by church leaders. This has created the recent trend for Old Order Mennonites to leave their ancestral homelands and relocate to distant communities in order to preserve the agrarian life.

Old Order Mennonite farming practices include more modern

technology than is typical of the Old Order Amish, but there are some restrictions. Tractors are permitted. However, they must have steel wheels.

Pneumatic rubber tires were forbidden about 1937 after Bishop Joseph Wenger observed the high rate of speed that tractors could travel on the roads. He believed rubber-tired tractors were the first step on the path to purchasing a truck which would inevitably lead to the desire for an automobile. Since the Groffdale Old Order Conference was established because of the belief that cars led people astray, Wenger and his followers decided that tractors should have steel wheels to prevent them being used for transportation. Other self-propelled farm implements came under this restriction.

When Groffdale Conference Mennonites started a new settlement in Ohio in 1973, their steel wheels created a problem with local officials who saw the destruction of their roads. Tensions ran high at first and it was even reported that several Mennonite farmers were the targets of gunshots although no one was ever hurt.

Woolwich Township Homes and Farms

From the very beginning, telephones were permitted at places of business among the Ontario Woolwich Mennonites, but it wasn't until 1989 that they were allowed in the homes of the members.

It is thought the first Woolwich Mennonite family to have electricity in the home was an elderly couple who moved to a house in town. Because of their feeble condition, the ministry thought it would be unsafe for the couple to use kerosene lamps so they allowed the use of electricity (or hydro, to use the Canadian term). This concession was made about 1920 and opened the way for others.

However, many Woolwich families still prefer to do without electricity, as well as modern plumbing and telephones. The general trend is not to install modern conveniences in old homes that have never had them, but new homes are equipped with the extras.

One of the biggest differences between the Groffdale and the Woolwich Mennonites is in farm equipment. Woolwich Mennonites make full use of tractors and implements with pneumatic tires. When these tires first made an appearance in the mid-1930s, the matter was discussed in the Woolwich Conference council but no final decision was made. Eventually, virtually all Woolwich

Both groups of Old Order Mennonites in Rockingham County, Virginia, have used tractors with pneumatic tires (shown here) for many years. This is also true of the Ontario Conference of Old Order Mennonites.

Mennonite farmers began using air tires on their tractors. Today, church rules caution against using them as road vehicles.

Virginia Conference Homes and Farms

Virtually all members of the larger group of Old Order Mennonites (Cline group) in Virginia make use of electricity. However, microwave ovens and air conditioners have not been approved. Most families still prefer old-style wringer washers and do not have electric dryers.

Virginia Old Orders had been using tractors with pneumatic tires for some time when the church divided in 1953. The Groffdale Conference advised the Russel Cline Group to change to steel wheels on their tractors, which was the Groffdale ruling. In the 1960s Rockingham County, Virginia, outlawed steel wheels on public roads. The Groffdale Conference gave the okay for the Virginians to go back to rubber tires.

Buggies

Those Old Order Mennonites who have not allowed car ownership have developed characteristic styles of horse-drawn vehicles in each of their major communities. Some of these are illustrated in the following pictures.

A *typical family carriage of the Groffdale (Old Order) Mennonite Conference is shown here. This same basic style is now used by most young folks in the group who had formerly used only buggies with folding tops.*

Until recently most Wenger Mennonite youth made use of buggies with fold-down tops. These have largely been replaced by carriages similar to those used by adults.

The vehicles of the Old Order Mennonites of Indiana are similar but not identical to their Pennsylvania kin.

The majority of Old Order Mennonites in Ontario use only open vehicles. Some older people do prefer carriages with stationary tops, however.

Virginia Old Order Mennonites had used only one- and two-seat folding top vehicles, but these are being largely replaced by vehicles with stationary tops.

TABLE THREE
The Smaller Old Order Mennonite Groups

David Martin Old Order Mennonites

Location: Waterloo County, Ontario—4 meetinghouses
Current Number: Possibly 400 or more members
Parent Group: Ontario Old Order Mennonite Conference
Date of Division: 1917
Number of People Involved in Original Division: 45
Initial Leader: Minister David B. Martin (1838-1920)
Reason for Division: Advocated a more rigid discipline, including the strict shunning of excommunicated members, a practice not generally held by Old Order Mennonites.
Differences in Practice from Parent Group: Shunning of excommunicated, electricity only from home generators, no tractors, no rubber tires, do not participate in the Ontario Old Order parochial schools, have arranged for special treatment from two different rural public schools which service their community. Men and women wear generally darker colors. Men's hats have wider brims. Women wear close fitting "Queen Victoria" bonnets year round rather than just in winter.
Additional Notes: Very active in cottage industries. Permitted telephones and self-generated electricity in the 1980s.
    The Daniel Brubacher Group divided from the Ontario (Old Order) Mennonite Conference in 1909 and joined the David Martin Group at its onset. In 1920 Brubacher, who had been made bishop, and some followers withdrew again and functioned as an independent group until 1962. Bishop Enoch Horst and a small group also withdrew from David Martin in 1924 and held preaching services until 1955.

Orthodox Mennonites (Huron County)

Alternate Name: Elam S. Martin Group, Gorrie Group
Location: Gorrie, Huron County, Ontario—2 meetinghouses
Current Number: Possibly 200 or more members.
Parent Group: David Martin Mennonites
Date of Division: 1953 (church organized 1957)
Initial Leader: Elam S. Martin (1907-)
Reason for Division: Concern about the spiritual condition of the church, encouraged reforms such as abstaining from the use of tobacco.
Differences in Practice from Parent Group: Maintain very conservative technology standards, no telephones, no propane gas, advocate high moral standards, operate their own parochial schools. Men wear beards and neither men nor boys wear neckties.
Additional Notes: In 1979 the entire Orthodox Mennonite community moved from Waterloo County, Ontario to Gorrie, Ontario. The Orthodox Mennonites work some what with the Noah Hoover Mennonite Group of Scottsville, Kentucky. After 1989 several families from the Ontario (Old Order) Mennnonite Conference joined the Orthodox Mennonites when the decision was made to permit telephones in the homes.

Orthodox Mennonites (Waterloo County)

Alternate Name: Elam M. Martin Group
Location: Waterloo County, Ontario—1 meetinghouse
Current Number: Probably fewer than 20 members
Parent Group: Orthodox Mennonites (Huron County)
Date of Division: 1974
Initial Leader: Anson Hoover (1920-)
Reason for Division: Many of the Orthodox Mennonite men started wearing beards after they began associating with the Noah Hoover Group (see Stauffer Mennonite groups). This became the central issue which divided the group.
Differences in Practice from Parent Group: Men do not wear beards.
Additional Notes: In 1976 this group divided again with the majority following Anson Hoover into the Conservative Mennonite Church of Ontario. A small remnant reorganized in the original Orthodox meetinghouse abandoned by the group which relocated in Huron County in 1979.

Reidenbach Old Order Mennonites

Alternate Name: Thirty-fivers, ten different sub-groups are each known by their leader's name - Amos Martin, John Martin, Ivan Hoover, Aaron Martin, Rufus Martin, Rufus Hoover, David Hoover, Earl Hoover, Henry Hoover, Peter Nolt.
Location:

Lancaster County, Pennsylvania	2 meetinghouses (1 shared by 2 groups), 5 house meetings
Morgan County, Missouri	1 house meeting
Christian County, Kentucky	1 house meeting
Montour/Northumberland Counties, Pennsylvania	1 meetinghouse

Numbers: Approximately 300 members divided into 10 sub-groups
Parent Group: Groffdale (Old Order) Mennonite Conference
Date of Division: 1942, organized as a separate group in 1946
Number of People Involved in Original Division: About 35
Initial Leader: David Hoover
Reason for Division: The progenitors of the Reidenbach Old Orders believed participation in Civilian Public Service camps for conscientious objectors during World War II represented compromise with the larger society. Instead they supported their young men's refusal to take part, resulting in jail terms for several of the men. They also opposed members' participation in the war time food ration stamp program. There was also a feeling that the Groffdale Conference was adopting too much modern technology.
Differences in Practice from Parent Group: Much more conservative position on technology, no tractors or other self-propelled machinery, no electricity, no telephones, and no rubber rims on buggy wheels. The Amos Martin Group makes use of propane gas and motorized horse drawn machinery, the other groups do not.

John Dan Wenger Group

Location: Rockingham County, Virginia—2 meetinghouses shared with Virginia (Old Order) Mennonite Conference
Current Number: Approximately 250 members
Parent Group: Virginia (Old Order) Mennonite Conference
Date of Division: 1952
Number of People Involved in Original Division: One-third of the membership of the Virginia Old Orders at the time.
Initial Leader: John Dan Wenger (1871-1967)

Reason for Division: Profound personality conflict between Bishop John Dan Wenger and Minister Russel Cline. When Wenger silenced Cline in 1952, two-thirds of the membership sided with Cline. The Groffdale, Ontario, and Ohio-Indiana Old Order Mennonite Conferences supported Cline.

Differences in Practice from Parent Group: No electricity.

Harvey Nolt Group

Location: Lancaster County, Pennsylvania and Richland County, Ohio
Parent Group: Groffdale (Old Order) Mennonite Conference
Date of Division: 1970
Number of People Involved in Original Division: Only a few
Initial Leader: Harvey Nolt (1919-1975)
Reason for Division: Harvey Nolt, a junior bishop, wanted to allow the use of pneumatic rubber tires on tractors. He withdrew from conference in opposition to the rulings against these items. Nolt was killed in a bicycle-car accident in 1975 and support for the new group he had started faltered.
Differences in Practice from Parent Group: Use of pneumatic rubber tires on tractors.
Current Number: Small group of loyal Nolt followers in Lancaster County which has affiliated itself with the John Dan Wenger Group in Virginia. Continue to attend regular Groffdale Conference services but do not partake in their communion services.
Expansion: Small group in Richland County, Ohio.

William Weaver Group

Location: Elkhart County, Indiana
Current Number: 55 members share the Groffdale Conference meetinghouses.
Parent Group: Groffdale (Old Order) Mennonite Conference (Indiana)
Date of Division: 1981
Initial Leader: Bishop William G. Weaver (1922-)
Reason for Division: Bishop William Weaver helped lead the Ohio-Indiana (Old Order) Mennonite Conference into the Groffdale Conference in 1971, but a decade later breached Groffdale rules by permitting pneumatic tires on small tractors used to clean out dairy barns. A division resulted with a minority remaining under the leadership of William Weaver in an independent group.
Differences in Practice from Parent Group: Use of pneumatic rubber tires on self-propelled farm equipment.
Additional Notes: This group has ties to both John Dan Wenger Group and the Harvey Nolt Group.

John Martin Group

Location:
Lancaster County, Pennsylvania—1 house meeting
Morgan County, Missouri—1 house meeting
Current Number: Probably fewer than 50 members
Parent Group: Groffdale (Old Order) Mennonite Conference
Date of Division: 1993
Initial Leader: Deacon John M. Martin (1929-)
Reason for Division: When a newly ordained minister refused to abide by the ruling which forbad electricity and telephones to the ordained, the regulation was changed. Deacon John M. Martin objected to the change as well as other trends he considered as drift and led a few families in Pennsylvania and Missouri out of the Groffdale Conference.
Differences in Practice from Parent Group: Ministry does not have electricity or telephones and generally more conservative in other ways.

3.
Traveling More Rapidly in the Straight and Narrow Way: The Automobile Old Order Mennonites

Those Old Order Mennonites who permitted the use of automobiles, telephones, and the English language organized three regional conferences (Ohio-Indiana, Weaverland, and Markham-Waterloo) between 1907 and 1931. Today, these conferences cooperate with each other in many ways, but, like their horse-and-buggy cousins, the car-driving Old Order Mennonites have no central church structure. In 1994 there were 45 congregations located in eight states and one Canadian province with a total membership of over 6,500 (see table 4).

Life and Faith

The Ohio-Indiana, Weaverland, and Markham-Waterloo Mennonite Conferences have retained the basic tenets of the Old Order Mennonite faith as upheld by Jacob Wisler, Jonas Martin, and Abraham Martin, the original leaders of the late 1800s Old Order movement. When the Old Order groups began having problems in the early 1900s leading to the formation of the car-driving Old Orders, the issues had changed. Instead of disputes over forms of worship and church activity, people were debating issues related to daily living, in particular questions about the rapid advances in technology.

The Old Order Mennonites who adopted cars continued to worship in the traditional manner, often sharing the same meetinghouses with their horse-and-buggy cousins. Such is the case at the Martindale meetinghouse in Lancaster County, Pennsylvania (*ca.* 1960).

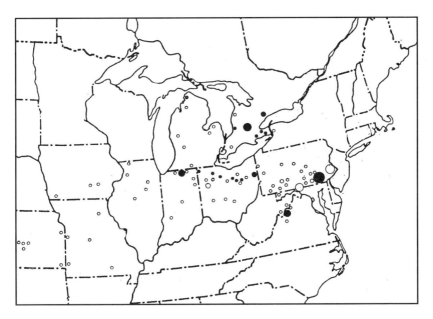

Automobile Old Order Mennonite Communities in 1996.

TABLE FOUR

The Automobile Old Order Mennonites

Ohio-Indiana (Wisler) Mennonite Conference

Alternate Names: Wisler Mennonites, Ramer Mennonites (in Indiana)
Numbers: Approximately 637 (estimated 1994)

Settlements	Founded	Meetinghouses
Elkhart County, Indiana	Original	2
Wayne County, Ohio	Original	1
Mahoning County, Ohio	Original	1
Sanilac County, Michigan	1981	1

History: The Old Order Mennonites of the Ohio-Indiana Conference divided into two factions in 1907. Nearly all the Old Orders in Ohio and the majority of the members in Indiana identified with the less traditional group which became known as Wisler Mennonites, a term sometimes used to refer to all Old Order Mennonites. Among the Old Orders themselves it is used only to refer to this group. Telephones and English preaching were the central issues in the division. The Wislers also approved automobile ownership in 1924. A large group of Wisler Mennonites in Ohio withdrew from the Ohio-Indiana Conference in 1973 and organized a separate Ohio Wisler Mennonite Conference, which eventually associated with the Eastern Pennsylvania Mennonite Church and other conservative Mennonite groups. The two remaining Wisler churches in Ohio continue to relate to the Ohio-Indiana Conference and other car-driving Old Order Mennonites.

Markham-Waterloo Mennonite Conference
Numbers: 1,106 members (1993)

Settlements	Founded	Meetinghouses
Waterloo, Wellington, and Perth Counties, Ontario	Original	8
York County, Ontario (Markham)	Original	1 (nearly extinct)
Haldimand-Norfolk County, Ontario (Rainham)	Original	extinct
Huron County, Ontario (Brotherston)	1974	1
Renfrew County, Ontario (Beachburg)	1980	1

History: The Old Order Mennonites at Markham and Rainham, Ontario, were dissassociated from the Ontario Old Order Mennonite Conference in 1931 for permitting car ownership, telephones, and English church services. A large group in Waterloo County withdrew from the Ontario Old Order Mennonite Conference in 1939 and joined with the Markham church to form the Markham-Waterloo Mennonite Conference.

Weaverland Mennonite Conference

Alternate Names: Horning Mennonites, Black Bumper Mennonites
Numbers: 4,767 members (1994)

Settlements	Founded	Meetinghouses
Lancaster County, Pennsylvania	Original	12
York County, Pennsylvania	Original	extinct
Lebanon and Berks Counties, Pennsylvania	1928	6
Rockingham County, Virginia	1957	1
Moniteau County, Missouri	1972	1
Scotland and Knox Counties, Missouri	1973	3
Seneca and Wayne Counties, New York	1976	2
Cumberland County, Pennsylvania	1978	1
Perry County, Pennsylvania	1979	1
Clark County, Wisconsin	1984	1
Snyder County, Pennsylvania	1985	1
Floyd County, Iowa	1986	1*

History: Moses Horning (1870-1955) became the junior bishop in the Weaverland Conference in 1914. When senior bishop Jonas Martin died in 1925, Horning refused to continue expelling members who owned cars. Those who wished to continue the ban on cars withdrew from the Weaverland Conference and organized the Groffdale Conference under the leadership of Joseph O. Wenger. Moses Horning's group retained the original Weaverland Conference name and about half of the members. At five of the original meetinghouses in Lancaster County, Pennsylvania, the Weaverland and Groffdale groups have taken turns having church services every other week. A few Old Order Mennonites in Virginia joined the Weaverland Conference after 1927, but no church was organized in that area until 1957.

* Worship in private homes

While the Ohio-Indiana, Weaverland, and Markham-Waterloo Conferences have permitted the use of cars, they do not view that as making them less Old Order because the ownership of cars was not an issue during the late 1800s break with the Mennonite Church. (Cars were not yet available.) The three car-driving Old Order conferences

While car-driving Old Order Mennonites have accepted modern technology for their homes and farms, they have retained the old ways in matters of worship. The scene above is a view from the nursery looking into the main assembly room of the Springville Mennonite Church (Weaverland Conference).

TABLE FIVE

Order of Worship for Automobile Old Orders

Weaverland Conference	Markham-Waterloo Conference	Ohio-Indiana Conference (Indiana order)
1. Three or four hymns (selected and announced by song leaders at singers' table)	1. Hymn announced by a minister (usually English)	1. Three hymns (selected by any-one in congregation, number repeated by a minister who reads the first stanza and then repeats the number)
2. Ministers come in on third or fourth hymn	2. Hymn announced by a song leader (sometimes German)	2. Opening sermon
3. Minister announces remaining hymn and reads the first stanza	3. Opening sermon	3. Silent prayer (all kneel)
4. Opening sermon	4. Silent prayer (all kneel)	4. Deacon reads text
5. Silent prayer (all kneel)	5. Deacon reads scripture	5. Main sermon
6. Deacon reads scripture	6. Main sermon	6. Testimonies from other ministers present
7. Main sermon	7. Testimonies from other ministers present	7. Hymn
8. Testimonies of other ministers present	8. Main speaker responds	8. Benediction (congregation sits)
9. Main speaker responds	9. Audible prayer (all kneel)	9. Announcements
10. Audible prayer (all kneel)	10. Hymn announced by song leader (usually German)	
11. Two hymns	11. Hymn announced by song leader (English)	
12. Announcements	12. Benediction (congregation sits)	
13. Benediction (standing)	13. Announcements	

The Yellowcreek (Wisler) Old Order Mennonite meetinghouse was originally built in 1861 before the Old Order division. From 1907 to 1912, three different groups shared the building but now only the Wisler (car-driving) group occupies it.

The Meadow Valley Weaverland Conference Mennonite Church near Ephrata, Pennsylvania, was originally built in 1916 but was added to in 1939, 1950, and 1982. It has the largest seating capacity of any church in the conference and had 310 members in 1995.

have also made a transition to English in their worship services. Again, there was always a degree of flexibility on the language issue. (For example, the Virginia Old Orders have always used English.)

Though they have modernized in some respects, the car-driving Old Orders retain the traditional forms of worship established at the time of the late 1800s break from the main body of Mennonites. They do not operate Sunday schools. Their leadership structures, ordination procedures, instruction classes for new members, baptism and communion services, funeral customs, and holidays observed are almost identical to the practices of the horse-and-buggy Mennonites with whom they parted ways in the early 1900s. This adherence to old forms of worship is the main factor which characterizes them as Old Order.

Weddings

While the car-driving Old Order Mennonites follow the same basic patterns of church life as the horse-and-buggy Old Orders, they have changed some of their wedding practices.

Most car Old Orders do not have weddings in church buildings, but many weddings are not held in the home of the bride either. In 1979 a

The Midway Reception Center in Lancaster County, Pennsylvania, was constructed in 1979 by Weaverland Conference Mennonites to provide a large facility for wedding receptions, which had traditionally been held in the homes. Today, many couples choose to hold both the wedding service and the reception at Midway.

group of Horning (Weaverland Conference) Mennonites independently constructed the Midway Reception Center near Lititz, Pennsylvania. This large building was initially used for wedding receptions, family gatherings, and young people's activities and was rented out for various other purposes. There was great resistance to having the actual wedding service in the facility, but this was finally permitted in 1988.[1] Since 1971 many weddings have also been held at the Fairmount Rest Home, operated by Weaverland Conference members[2].

Some wedding customs associated with the Groffdale Conference Mennonites have been dropped by the Weaverland Conference people. Wine and cookies are rarely served to guests at a Weaverland

The responsibility of homemaking is taken very seriously by women in the car-driving Old Order Mennonite groups. Despite the extra mobility provided by cars, very few mothers have outside jobs.

wedding. Neither do the young men and women assemble in separate rooms before the wedding. The bride most often wears a light blue dress but, with the exception of white, other colors are also seen. If a wedding is held at a place other than the bride's home, there is usually no afternoon singing. Unlike their horse-and-buggy cousins, the car-driving Old Orders do not continue the wedding reception through an evening meal.

In the Markham-Waterloo Conference most weddings are held at the home of the bride. The wedding dress is always blue. The Indiana Wisler Mennonites began holding weddings in meetinghouses in 1969. This transition had occurred somewhat earlier in Ohio. White wedding dresses have been the norm in Ohio and Indiana for many years.

Transportation

The Old Order Mennonites who accepted cars did so with some stipulations. When cars were permitted by the Weaverland Conference in 1927, members were required to purchase black touring cars with all the chrome or nickel trim also painted black. The touring car with its fold-down top and detachable side curtains was originally preferred because it was the least expensive model of automobile. By the time the Weaverland Conference allowed cars, the touring car was somewhat old-fashioned. Today, it would probably be considered a sporty convertible, but the Old Orders and other people of that time did not think of it in that way.

About 1933 the new touring cars offered by the automobile companies were unacceptable to the Horning Mennonites because of their sporty, light colored tops rather than plain black ones. The Weaverland conference finally permitted "out of style" closed cars (sedans) in 1935. For a few years before this, some enterprising car dealers went to the expense of bringing in acceptable plain touring cars from distant places and sold them to Mennonites at premium prices. After the ruling was changed, the dealers were stuck with some expensive touring cars that few people wanted.

The Weaverland Conference modified its rule on completely black cars in 1945 and required only that the bumpers on cars be painted black and not necessarily the other trim.

In 1957 a number of Old Order Mennonites in Virginia were taken into the Weaverland Conference with the provision that they would

The Weaverland Old Order Mennonite Conference has insisted that all cars be black. Until 1957 all members were also required to paint chrome bumpers black; a practice still observed by the ministry as well as some other non-ordained members.

not need to paint their bumpers black. This opened the door for those in Pennsylvania who did not wish to continue the black bumper practice. Currently, less than half of Weaverland Conference vehicles have black bumpers although it is still required that all cars be painted black (which is true of all three car Old Order conferences). Ordained men in the Weaverland and Markham-Waterloo conferences drive black bumper cars. This had also been the practice in the Ohio-Indiana Conference, but the last ordained man to observe it died in 1983.

Even though black bumpers are no longer mandatory, the Weaverland Conference still regulates the types of cars its members may own. In 1994 the Vehicle Aid Plan, maintained by conference members for liability coverage on cars, published a list of 64 sports cars and truck models which were not acceptable, 29 models which were considered marginal, and twelve luxury car makes and models which were strongly discouraged.

Car models that are only available with two doors and those that are limited to two passengers are considered sports cars and hence unacceptable. Convertibles, T roofs, and sun roofs are prohibited, along with high powered engines in small cars. Trucks and vans are not to be multi-colored. All vehicles used to come to church or social activities are to be black.[3]

Dress standards among car-driving Old Order Mennonites follow traditional patterns. Women wear large head coverings with tie strings and cape dresses. They often wear black bonnets outdoors, especially to church. Men's dress practices vary somewhat, but black hats and plain coats are typical. The people shown here are from the Markham-Waterloo Conference in Ontario, but are fairly typical of other car-driving Old Order Mennonites.

Girls in the Weaverland Old Order Mennonite Conference begin wearing head coverings in their mid-teens. White tie strings are exchanged for black ones after marriage. Men are clean shaven and have closely cropped hair. Plain black hats are worn for more formal occasions, but bill caps are typical for everyday work.

Church Standards

The car Old Orders have few restrictions on technology but do forbid radio and television. Tape players and other such entertainment devices are discouraged. Photographs had been cautioned against but are now quite common. Picture taking at weddings is still forbidden. Modern farm machinery is no problem for any of the three conference groups.

The Ohio-Indiana and Markham-Waterloo Conferences forbid tobacco use among members. In the Weaverland Conference, where many members have traditionally grown tobacco, smoking is discouraged but not made a test of membership.

Education

The majority of children from car Old Order homes attend parochial schools operated by the churches. The Indiana Wisler churches bought a relatively large public school building where the 200 plus students have a separate room for each of the ten grades and also a special education class.

Most Markham-Waterloo children go to schools jointly operated with the horse-and-buggy Woolwich Old Order Mennonites. Some also attend rural public schools, which are predominately Mennonite in constituency.

Beginning in the 1960s, the Weaverland and Groffdale Conference Mennonites cooperated in operating their own schools under the Old Order Amish plan. Some Horning Mennonites started a separate organization called Weaverland Schools in 1978. These schools generally have three or more rooms and make use of curriculum materials from conservative Mennonite publishers. The schools extend to ninth grade with a few going to tenth. For those who wish to take high school work, a home school program is provided in which students report to one of the schools once a month. In Lancaster County, the majority of Horning students attend one of the six schools in the Weaverland system. The Lebanon County Horning Mennonites operate twelve one- and two-room schools under the Old Order plan.

Since the 1960s, a few young people from car Old Order church-

Farmersville Mennonite School, begun in 1978 in a former public school building, was the first of six schools started by the Weaverland Mennonite Schools organization in Pennsylvania.

es have attended high schools run by other Mennonite groups. An even smaller number of youth from this group have graduated from college.

Youth Activities

Youth in the Markham-Waterloo and Ohio-Indiana churches gather in the homes of members for Sunday evening singings. They also engage in informal ballgames, skating, and other social activities.

This pattern was also true of Weaverland Conference youth until about the 1970s when the sheer size of the youth group seemed to warrant a more structured organization. The majority of Horning Mennonite young people became involved in the Youth for Truth, which elects three boys and three girls to serve on a committee. This group has a charity project every year to grow produce for the Fairmount Home and other worthy causes. It is called charity acres. Other activities include social events such as spelling bees.

Many youth in the conservative Lebanon County district are not involved with Youth for Truth and continue the traditional Sunday evening singings in the homes of the members. The Weaverland Conference also sponsors a song service at one of the meeting-houses every weekend. Each congregation has a committee of parents that plans youth activities such as "supper crowds."

Language

Nearly all sermons among car-driving Old Order Mennonites are conducted in the English language. Some ministers in the Markham-Waterloo Conference prefer to give testimony in German, and a few Weaverland ministers may begin their sermons in German. In Markham-Waterloo churches at least one German hymn is still sung at every worship service. This was also the custom among the Indiana Wisler Mennonites until 1948. In the Weaverland Conference, the Lebanon County churches continued the practice until 1976. A German hymn is still sung at Lebanon County communion services. The Wisler Mennonites in Ohio and Indiana were the first to make the transition from German to English in church, which occurred largely in the early 1900s.

In the Weaverland Conference, few people born after about 1960 speak the Pennsylvania German dialect at home, as is true in Indiana and Ohio. Among Markham-Waterloo people, Pennsylvania

German is still commonly spoken by all ages.

All car-driving Old Order Mennonites, except one congregation in Ohio, make use of A *Collection of Psalms and Hymns* (Mennonite Hymns) for congregational singing. This book descends from the first major English language Mennonite hymnal originally published in Virginia in 1847. These small books have no musical notation. The tunes are designated by poetic meter.

Occupations

Farming is still the preferred occupation among members of the Ohio-Indiana, Markham-Waterloo, and Weaverland Conferences. Many members have also gone into various businesses and have often been quite successful.

In 1937 Edwin Nolt, a Weaverland Conference member, invented a hay baler which automatically tied the bales with twine as it was pulled through the field. Nolt built a baler production factory, but after selling 100 balers, he decided the business had become more than he wanted to handle.

In 1940 the Nolt Baler operation was sold to the New Holland Machine Company, and Edwin Nolt's invention became the proto-type for all modern hay balers. The tiny New Holland Machine operation grew into a multi-national farm equipment company—Ford

To provide for the elderly of their own church and those of the community, Weaverland Conference Mennonites founded Fairmount Rest Home near Ephrata, Pennsylvania, in 1968.

New Holland—which still has its corporate offices in New Holland, the small Pennsylvania town where Nolt, a car-driving Old Order Mennonite, built the very first New Holland baler.[4]

Organizations

The Weaverland Mennonite Conference does not have any official programs or agencies beyond the operation of the individual congregations. There are, however, a number of unofficial organizations which are supported and administered by Weaverland Conference members. Fairmount Home, Weaverland Mennonite Schools, the Vehicle Aid Plan, and the Mennonite Aid Ordinance have the full support of the ministry. There is also a Mission Interest Committee that collects and disburses funds to various missions and a mission work in Haiti that functions with non-ordained

The Weaverland Old Order Mennonite Conference has always taken a firm stand on conscientious objection to war. In this 1941 picture, three Weaverland Conference representatives and an Old Order Amishman consult with General Lewis B. Hershey, Director of Selective Service, concerning the draft. (Left to right) Bishop Joseph Hostetter (1890-1961 Weaverland Conference), Aaron Esh (Amish), General Lewis B. Hershey, Elam Hoover (1879-1954, Weaverland Conference) and John O. Huber (1877-1944, Weaverland Conference).

Weaverland Conference leadership. Many Weaverland members are also involved with Christian Aid Ministries, a relief and mission organization supported by Old Order and conservative Mennonite groups, as well as various Amish groups.

An unofficial newsletter called *The Home Messenger* was started by Weaverland Conference Mennonites in 1964. The Home Messenger Library, under the auspices of the publication, was started in 1995 in Ephrata, Pennsylvania, to provide Christian books and a repository for Mennonite historical materials.

The Church Correspondent has been published for the Markham-Waterloo Conference since 1955 and the *Exchange Messenger* began about the same time for Indiana Wisler Mennonites.

4.
An Old Road
with Many Branches:
The Stauffer Mennonites

In 1840 (some years before the main Old Order Mennonite division in Lancaster County) the seeds for another group, which would also eventually become horse-and-buggy Old Orders, were planted. A 28-year-old man named Jacob Stauffer was ordained to the ministry in the Groffdale district of the Lancaster Conference Mennonites (not to be confused with the later Groffdale [Wenger] Old Order Mennonite Conference). Despite his young age, Stauffer was a staunch conserva-

Jacob Stauffer withdrew from the Lancaster Mennonite Conference in 1845 and began a new group which met at the Pike meetinghouse near Ephrata, Pennsylvania. These people have been known as both Stauffer Mennonites and Pike Mennonites.

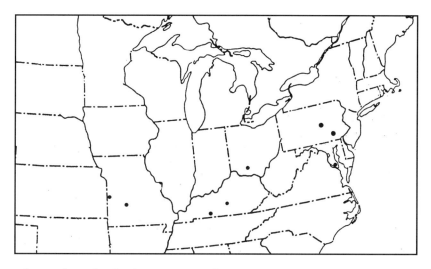

The Stauffer and Related Mennonite Settlements in 1996.

tive. He concluded there had been major backsliding in the church during the decade previous to his ordination and came to believe a more rigid discipline should be reinstated. Two incidents especially supported Stauffer's charges and helped to bring about his break with the Lancaster Conference Mennonites.[1]

The first episode occurred sometime in the early 1840s when the neighbors of a wealthy Mennonite couple observed them severely mistreating an orphan girl they had indentured. After the civil authorities were called to take care of the matter, the guilty party agreed to pay the girl when she came of age to make up for any harm they may have done her. The abusive couple was not excommunicated from the Mennonite Church until the law had become involved—a major point of contention with Jacob Stauffer.

When the girl reached the age of 18, the foster father refused to give her the money he had promised. He took the matter to court but lost the case. When the litigation was over, the conference moderator, Christian Herr, advised that the offending couple be received back into membership of the Groffdale Mennonite Church after a simple confession. Stauffer charged that they were treated as if they were only minor offenders, and the grave nature of their sin was not taken seriously. All of this deserved more than a mild reprimand, Stauffer contended. He also found the widespread support for the couple within the church difficult to accept.

The Stauffer Mennonites in Snyder County, Pennsylvania, met in homes for worship until a meetinghouse was built in 1870. This building (shown here) has been added to five times to accommodate a growing membership. There was no singers' table in the original small building, but when the building was expanded, this piece (center of photo) of traditional furniture was built for the meetinghouse and placed in front of the preachers' table.

As bad as this case was, it was really a second issue that caused the rift between Stauffer and the Lancaster Conference Mennonites. In 1845 the newly married daughter of a prominent Groffdale member fled to her parents' home, charging her husband with cruelty. The enraged father, his daughter, and two sons brought the matter to the local justice of the peace who issued a warrant for the spouse's arrest. The family of the girl and a host of neighbors accompanied by the constable went to the home of the accused and began loading up the daughter's furniture.

The hapless husband returned during the disruption, and a chase ensued when the armed constable and several others pursued the man for nearly a mile before he gave up. On the way home the men with the loaded wagons stopped at an inn and the father paid his helpers with several rounds of drinks. The merry party could be heard for miles around as they jubilantly shouted and cheered on their return home.

Feeling some remorse for his actions, the father later saw to it that a signed and witnessed statement was drawn up by the justice of

This meetinghouse in Snyder County, Pennsylvania, is shared by the Joseph Brubaker and Allen Martin Groups. They take turns with each group meeting every other Sunday.

the peace in which the wife was not to have legal right to the possessions and wealth of the husband and vice versa.

All this caused quite a furor in the Groffdale Church. On September 14, 1845, Bishop Christian Herr was again brought in as an arbitrator. The father of the estranged wife appeared before the church and made a long confession of his wrongdoing. After the apology, Bishop Herr proclaimed, "I hope you can tolerate him thus in love and peace."[2]

A major part of the church was in favor of accepting the man's confession with no furthur discipline. Jacob Stauffer and a minority thought that the offense was serious enough to warrant expulsion and the ban. The second alternative was sternly resisted by Bishop Herr who pled for mercy. There was a heated discussion as the 34-year-old Stauffer locked horns with the 65-year-old Herr. The meeting ended without a clear decision.

Stauffer could not with good conscience accept Herr's recommendation. Not only had the father's sin been treated lightly, but other members of the family also involved in the fracas were not even mentioned by Bishop Herr or the Groffdale ministry. To Stauffer the primary transgression was calling the constable and involving the law of the land. He saw this as entirely opposed to the Mennonite doctrine of non-resistance. He also regarded the agreement between the estranged husband and wife as a divorce. Stauffer could not understand why Bishop Herr would call this "a nice friendly writing"[3] when it was so contrary to Mennonite practice.

Jacob Stauffer's refusal to accept Bishop Herr's counsel caused more indignation in the church than the original offense. Christian Herr (1780-1853) was a highly respected bishop in the Lancaster Mennonite Conference. He was a gifted speaker and writer and several of his hymns were published in hymnbooks used by the Mennonites.

The majority of the congregation agreed that Stauffer should not only be set back from communion and counsel but should also give up his ministry. Ultimately Stauffer and about 50 supporters were expelled from the church. Stauffer's followers were permitted to use the Pike meetinghouse of the Groffdale congregation, located on the Harrisburg-Downingtown Turnpike (which later became Route 322). Because of the use of this meetinghouse, the Stauffer Mennonites have commonly been called Pikers.

Bishop Jacob Brubacher of Juniata County, Pennsylvania, was also expelled from the Lancaster Mennonite Conference when he expressed disagreement with Christian Herr's decision. Consequently, a congregation of Stauffer sympathizers was established in the Juniata-Snyder County area.

Distinctive Beliefs of the Stauffer or Pike Mennonites

In 1848 Jacob Stauffer published A *Foundation of Faith and Confession,* giving a detailed explanation and defense of his doctrines and practices. The ten articles in this writing forbade serving in "worldly offices, serving as a juryman in civil court, voting in civil elections, becoming a member of a mutual insurance company, attending worldly meetings and conventions, arresting or suing a person, making use of civil force, installing and using lightning rods, attending camp meetings and singing schools, taking insurance among the brethren for money or property (surety, bail, mortgage or judgment), cutting or combing hair after the fashions of the world, and dressing in worldly fashions and ornaments, including doubled or cutaway coats [probably referring to lapels or double breasted and tail coats]."[4] This list was followed by a detailed explanation of each point with supporting scriptural principles.

A separate article was devoted to the "Withdrawal from or Shunning of Apostate and Separated Members." Stauffer began this section by saying, "This doctrine has been lost among the so-called [Mennonite] church but is again observed by us."[5]

Jacob Stauffer was obviously concerned about much more than just the issues involved in the two incidents at Groffdale. He saw a general worldly trend in the Mennonite Church which included political involvement, social involvement, involvement with other religious groups, involvement with insurance (including lightning rods), and involvement with fashion.

The Stauffer Mennonites Today

Since their beginnings in 1845, the Stauffer Mennonites have divided into several different groups. The largest group is usually referred to as the Stauffer Mennonite Church or the Jacob Stauffer Group. They take their name from Jacob S. Stauffer, a grandson and namesake of the group's founder. Jacob S. Stauffer was bishop of the Lancaster County congregation from 1933 to 1987.

The Jacob Stauffer Group has experienced gradual growth over the years with a recent significant increase. In 1977 there were 382[6] members which increased to 700[7] in 1990. For many years, Stauffer young people typically "sowed their wild oats," engendering the label "Wild Pikers." Most usually waited until after marriage to join the church, and many never affiliated with the church of their parents.

Since the early 1970s, much more emphasis has been placed on living a consistent Christian life as a youth. Therefore, the trend has changed, and a much higher percentage of young people have been joining the church in their late teens and early twenties.

Today, the Jacob Stauffer Group has expanded beyond the original communities in Lancaster and Snyder Counties in Pennsylvania. New settlements were established at Loveville, Maryland, in 1940; Tunas, Missouri, in 1969; Elkhorn, Kentucky, in 1987; and Bainbridge, Ohio, in 1989.

While the Jacob Stauffer Group of Snyder County, Pennsylvania, was extinct for a time in the 1940s and 50s due to schism, it was reestablished when some of the folks from a splinter group returned to the original church and people from Lancaster County moved to the area. The Jacob Stauffer membership in Snyder County today is nearly equal to that of Lancaster. A second meetinghouse was built there in the 1980s.

A small number of the Noah Hoover Group in Snyder County, Pennsylvania, were still meeting for worship in this schoolhouse (top) in 1995. The majority of the group had moved to Scottsville, Kentucky, in 1978. This scene (bottom) captures the departure of one contingent as they left Pennsylvania in a chartered bus.

Divisions among the Stauffer Mennonites

As is the case with many ultra-conservative Christian groups, the Stauffer Mennonites have had a great many controversies on where exactly to draw the line between the church and the world. The first dispute came within the first decade after Jacob Stauffer's 1845 break with the Lancaster Conference Mennonites.

Daniel Brubaker—the son of Bishop Jacob H. Brubacher, a staunch supporter of Jacob Stauffer—was ordained bishop of the Juniata-Snyder County congregation. By 1857 Daniel Brubaker had broken fellowship with the Stauffer Mennonites because he wished to take a somewhat more liberal path. All the members in Juniata County and some of those in Snyder County followed Daniel Brubaker and operated independently until 1897 when then Bishop Jacob B. Weaver effected a merger with the newly formed Weaverland Conference of Old Order Mennonites. Jacob Weaver and most of the Daniel Brubaker group moved to Lancaster County and were assimilated into what became the larger body of Old Order Mennonites.[8]

Many divisions among the Stauffer Mennonites created a collec-

Stauffer Mennonites are exceptional in the degree of simplicity and conservatism that characterizes every area of their lives. Very plain horse drawn vehicles and dress are part of this emphasis.

tion of groups all of whom fit under the Stauffer umbrella. Some have become extinct. Some such as the Daniel Brubaker group have been assimilated into other Mennonite groups. Some still operate as independent congregations (see table 5 for a listing of these groups.)

Very wide-brimmed hats and center-parted or banged hair that is cut off straight in the back are characteristic of Stauffer Mennonite men. Work coats as well as suitcoats must have standing collars. The men with narrower-brimmed hats in this farm auction photo are probably Wenger Mennonites.

The Separated Life

The Mennonite groups stemming from the 1845 Stauffer division are the most conservative part of the Swiss Mennonite family outside of the Amish. In many ways the Stauffer-related Mennonites closely resemble the Amish. All of the Stauffer groups forbid the ownership and driving of cars and limit technology much like the Amish. The very plain clothing of the Stauffer Mennonites is comparable to the Amish style. However, unlike the Amish, Stauffer men wear buttons on their coats and vests instead of hooks and eyes. Also the men in most Stauffer-related groups are clean shaven. Amish men, of course, wear beards. (The Titus Hoover and Noah Hoover groups adopted the wearing of beards through influence from the Amish.)

Stauffer-related women usually wear subdued colors, but small printed fabric is permitted. White head coverings cover the ears and are tied beneath the chin. In the Jacob Stauffer Group black tie strings were introduced about 1910 and have nearly replaced the older white style.[9] Shawls and large black bonnets are the rule for weather protection.

Stauffer Mennonite women wear shawls and large bonnets outdoors during cold weather.

Stauffer Mennonite children are dressed in the traditional plain garb of the group. In the past, most Stauffer teenagers dressed in more stylish dress before they became church members. Today, fewer youth go through this rebellious stage.

It had been the practice in the Jacob Stauffer Group for the parents to insist that their children dress according to the standards of the church until age sixteen after which the choice of how to dress was left largely to the individual. In the past most young women began dressing like more modern car-driving conservative Mennonites when they became teenagers. Since the 1970s a large percentage of young people have continued wearing the traditional clothing of the church after age sixteen and have been baptized while still in their teens and before marriage.

Stauffer Mennonite meetinghouses follow the styles and patterns of the Groffdale Old Order Mennonite Conference (see chapter 2). One difference is that the original Pike meetinghouse of Lancaster County still has a completely enclosed barn which was formerly used to shelter horses that were ridden to church.

The Stauffer Mennonites use the same German hymnal as the Groffdale Conference Old Order Mennonites. They also sing basically the same tunes but at a considerably slower pace. One also

Stauffer Mennonite children attend one-room schools, completing grades one through eight.

hears fewer English words in the preaching at Stauffer services than among the Groffdale Conference churches.

In Lancaster County the Stauffer Mennonites cooperate with other Old Order Mennonites in operating parochial schools. In Snyder County some of the groups have their own exclusive schools while others work together in maintaining schools. In all the smaller settlements parochial elementary schools have been established. Stauffer children terminate their education after the eighth grade.

Most of the Stauffer-related groups use horse drawn carriages which have no windows except the front windshield or storm front. The vehicles are black and have sliding doors. Compared to the carriages of the Groffdale Conference Mennonites, the Stauffer vehicles have a more square shape. Unlike the Groffdale Conference Mennonites, Stauffer young people drive open buggies with no dashboards.

The Weaver group (see page 101) began using steel wheeled tractors for field work and electricity in the homes many years ago. Electricity or tractors for field work are not used in the Jacob Stauffer Group, but propane gas for cooking and refrigeration is permitted.

Horse drawn farm machinery is the rule in nearly all Stauffer Mennonite groups.

Hot water heaters, pneumatic and hydraulic tools, and motorized horse drawn hay balers are innovations that have been accepted by the Jacob Stauffer Group. None of the other groups descending from the 1845 division (Aaron Martin, Titus Hoover, Noah Hoover, Joseph Brubaker, and Allen Martin) allow any of the modernizations just mentioned. The Noah Hoover Group goes further in not permitting any kind of internal combustion engine.

TABLE SIX
The Smaller Stauffer Mennonite Groups[10]

The Bowman/Rissler Group

Location: Snyder County, Pennsylvania
Numbers: 2 members (no ministry)
History: Minister Samuel Bowman left the Stauffer Mennonite Church in Lancaster County in 1866 when the original rule against allowing disobedient children to live at home was changed. Bowman's small group met for worship in homes until 1916 when they were invited back to the Stauffer group to provide leadership after the Weaver division. With Philip Rissler as their bishop, the Bowman element left the Stauffers again in 1920 and resumed house meetings until 1977 when the last minister died, leaving only two members who soon moved to Snyder County.

The Weaver Group

Location: Lancaster County, Pennsylvania (the Pike meetinghouse is shared with the Stauffer Mennonite Group)
History: The Stauffer Mennonite Church in Lancaster County divided in 1916. The controversy centered around the reinstatement of a young man without his wife becoming a member. (He had been expelled for marrying outside the church.) The more tolerant group became identified with John A. Weaver who became bishop in 1928.

A small group withdrew from the Ontario Mennonite Conference in 1884 and joined the Stauffer Mennonite Church. These people relocated to Osceola County, Iowa, in 1887. By 1915 most had moved back east to Lebanon County, Pennsylvania. The majority of the Lebanon County group sided with the Weaver Group of the 1916 division, but in 1928 the congregation joined the Weaverland Mennonite Conference.

The majority of the Weaver Group withdrew from the leadership of Bishop Martin B. Weaver in 1987 when he would not permit telephones. Deacon Jonas M. Weaver became the leader of the larger, more liberal group. The Jonas Weaver faction continued having services in the morning at the Pike meetinghouse while the few followers of Martin Weaver had a brief service in the afternoon.

The Phares Stauffer Group

Location: Formerly in Snyder County, Pennsylvania, and Lancaster County, Pennsylvania.

Numbers: Extinct

History: Minister Phares O. Stauffer of the Snyder County Stauffer Mennonite Church was strongly opposed to the food ration stamps issued during World War II. In 1944 Phares Stauffer and most of the members in Snyder County and a few from Lancaster County separated from the other Stauffer Mennonites on this issue. All but a few in the Phares Stauffer Group withdrew under the leadership of Joseph B. Stauffer in 1946. In 1967 there were only seven members reported. When Phares Stauffer died in 1992 at the age of 89, the remaining members disbanded.

The Aaron Martin Group

Location: Snyder County, Pennsylvania (share the Upper Snyder County meetinghouse with the Stauffer Mennonite Church)

Numbers: 45 members in 1995

History: Bishop Phares Stauffer was accused of failure when he didn't carry out proper disciplinary measures against three women, who independently and unknown to each other wore men's pants to help with the grain harvest of 1945. The ensuing controversy culminated in the great majority of members withdrawing from the Phares Stauffer Group in 1946. Aaron S. Martin was ordained a minister in this group and soon became bishop.

The Joseph Stauffer Group

Location: Formerly in Snyder County, Pennsylvania

Numbers: Merged with Stauffer Mennonite Church

History: Minister Joseph Stauffer, who had been ordained in the Phares Stauffer Group in 1944, and a few families left the Aaron Martin Group in 1951. Stauffer was somewhat less conservative in some material matters than Martin, and there were also some doctrinal differences. After meeting as a separate group for a short time, the Joseph Stauffer Group returned to the Stauffer Mennonite Church in 1953, thus reestablishing the group in Snyder County. Because of various divisions, the Stauffer Mennonite Church had been extinct in Snyder County for eight years. Joseph's original ordination was not recognized, but he was later ordained a minister and a bishop in the Snyder County Stauffer Church.

Titus Hoover Group

Alternate names: Church of God, Taufgesinnte (a German term for Anabaptist)
Location: Snyder County, Pennsylvania
Numbers: Fewer than ten.
History: Deacon Jonas Nolt of the Aaron Martin Group objected to growing and using tobacco and spoke out against what he considered modern farm machinery: hay loaders, manure spreaders, and corn binders. He also felt strongly that chicks should be hatched by brooding hens rather than bought from a hatchery. While only a few members followed Jonas Nolt out of the Aaron Martin Group in 1949, many more followed over the next five years. Titus B. Hoover was chosen minister and later bishop in the new group, thus superseding Jonas Nolt as the leader. In 1952 a group that had been affiliated with the Reformed Amish Christian Church in Tennessee (stemming from the group started by David Schwartz in Indiana in 1895) joined with Titus Hoover. Hoover forwarded the idea that his little band of people represented the "one true church." Other people of Amish background joined the Hoovers. However, many of these folks had left the group by 1957.

Many other members left in 1954 with Jonas Nolt and in 1963 with Noah Hoover. Titus Hoover was left for the most part with just the members of his own family. In 1969 there were nine members. Gradually, the Titus Hoover Group was again built up by people from diverse backgrounds, but a major rift over a lawsuit in 1995 left Titus and his wife alone. Titus stopped having services at this time. About half the former members went to the Noah Hoover group. Most of the others were undecided as to their affiliation. Around six people continued to adhere to the teachings of Titus Hoover, but under the leadership of Aron Peters.

Jonas Nolt Group

Location: The community at Lobelville, Tennessee, is in part descended from the Jonas Nolt Group.
History: Deacon Jonas Nolt felt that too many concessions were made for the people from the Reformed Amish Christian Church who joined the Titus Hoover Group in 1952. Nolt finally left the Titus Hoover group about 1954 and established a community at Mammoth Springs, Arkansas, in 1955. People of Mennonite, Amish, and German Baptist background were attracted to this ultra-orthodox group. The Arkansas community disbanded in the 1970s, but many of the members established a similar settlement at Lobelville, Tennessee.

Noah Hoover Group

Location: Snyder County, Pennsylvania (original) but all members planned to relocate in 1995
   Scottsville, Kentucky, founded 1978
   Rich Hill, Missouri, founded 1993
Numbers: Approximately 300 members
History: Minister Noah Hoover and the majority of members left the Titus Hoover Group in 1963 in rejection of Titus Hoover's doctrine of the one true church. Many people from various backgrounds have been attracted to the Noah Hoover Group. The ultra-conservative stance on technology combined with firm Biblicism, intense spirituality, and high moral standards have had a wide appeal. The Noah Hoover Group has fellowship with the Mennonite group at Upper Barton Creek in the country of Belize. There is also some relationship with the Orthodox Mennonites of Gorrie, Ontario. A related group was located at Monterey, Tennessee, but the few remaining members are not organized as a church.

The Joseph Brubaker Group

Location: Snyder County, Pennsylvania (share a meetinghouse with the Allen Martin Group)
   Lancaster County, Pennsylvania (meet in homes)
Numbers: 58 members in 1995
History: In a controversy centered on the alleged inconsistency of the bishop in applying church discipline, Minister Joseph O. Brubaker and a few members from Lancaster County and a larger number from Snyder County withdrew from the Stauffer Mennonite Church in 1962. The Brubaker Group stressed more rigid standards related to non-conformity to the world than did the larger Stauffer Group.

The Allen Martin Group

Location: Snyder County, Pennsylvania (share a meetinghouse with the Joseph Brubaker Group)
Numbers: 37 members in 1995
History: Minister Allen Z. Martin of the Joseph Brubaker Group favored allowing chainsaws and some other technological changes, which were not tolerated by Bishop David Brubaker. Martin also did not agree with the decision to shun a certain young couple who left the church (although the Brubaker Group does not necessarily shun all those who leave their church). The two factions that developed divided in 1976 with the smaller group following Allen Martin who became bishop of the new group.

5.
The First Keepers
of the Old Way:
The Reformed Mennonites

In about the year 1785, a Lancaster County Mennonite layperson named Francis Herr (1748-1810) stood before the ministerial body of the Lancaster Mennonite Conference and voiced his concern about the worldly drift of the church. Francis' father, minister John Herr, initially supported his son's views, but after counsel with the other ministers urged, "We must give way to our brethren; we cannot stand against them."[1] Francis, however, felt he could not compromise what he believed were important scriptural principles so he left the Mennonite Church.

Francis Herr thought that the Mennonite Church had become degenerate. He observed Mennonites, including the ordained, engaging in frivolous activities. He stated that some Mennonites had even been involved in public drunkenness. On doctrinal matters, Herr accused the Mennonites of departing from the teachings of Menno Simons and failing to observe such practices as feet washing, the holy kiss, and avoiding the excommunicated. He was also concerned about Mennonite participation in political elections.

Francis Herr soon gained a group of followers who assembled for informal worship at his house. Since Herr had not been ordained, he ministered to the people while seated as an act of humility. The group continued worshiping together after Herr's death in 1810.

Francis Herr also had a son named John Herr (1781-1850), who had grown up attending his father's informal meetings. As a young married man, he experienced conversion and began following the teachings of his father. After Francis Herr's death, John received a

In the years after the Mennonites settled in North America, the Reformed Mennonites were the first group to break away from the main body of the Mennonite Church. They wanted to maintain and restore the old ways. Very conservative plain dress has been maintained by this group. Even today Reformed Mennonite women's garb preserves 18th century Mennonite details not observed by any other of the plain Mennonite groups.

vision in which Christ told him to organize a church.

On May 30, 1812, the first meeting of this new church was held at John Herr's home near Strasburg, Pennsylvania. Herr was elected as the group's first pastor and bishop. Abraham Landis, who was called to serve as a minister, was asked to re-baptize John Herr who in turn re-baptized Landis.

At the group's next meeting, twenty-five people were baptized when they met at the home of David Buckwalter. Soon after this, John Herr's mother also was re-baptized along with sixteen more people. Later the same year, a commodious meetinghouse was built on the property of John Longenecker, very close to the old Francis Herr home.[2]

The John Herr group came to be called New Mennonites or Herrites. Some years after their initial organization, they officially adopted the name Reformed Mennonite Church. They saw themselves as the only true followers of Menno Simons' teachings.

Although they are not part of the Old Order Mennonite movement, the Reformed Mennonites are included here because they have much in common with the Old Orders. In some ways, the Reformed Mennonites have characteristics of both the Old Order and the later conservative Mennonites. In many other ways, they are very different from any other Mennonite group.

One True Church

Reformed Mennonites feel very strongly that there can be only one true church of Christ. They interpret Ephesians 4:4-6—"There is one body, and one Spirit, even as ye are called in one hope of your calling; One Lord, one faith, one baptism, One god and Father of all"—literally. They are convinced that the ". . . Scriptures should make it clear that there is but one visible, undivided church."[3] They further explain that all true followers of Christ will be drawn into unity and fellowship by Christian love.

An extension of the one true church doctrine is their doctrine of "separation from unfaithful worship." This means that church members do not attend the worship services of any other church group. Since other religious groups "do not live in harmony with the doctrines of Christ," Reformed Mennonites "do not want to encourage anyone in a course at variance with Christ's teachings."[4]

Prime concerns of the Reformed Mennonites are the unity and purity of the church. It is their desire to maintain a church "not having spot or wrinkle" (Ephesians 5:27). Those who break the precious unity of the church are dealt with according to the directives of Matthew 18. If the person remains recalcitrant, then he or she is brought before the church. If confession and repentance do not happen, the church puts the person under the ban, following a literal understanding of the scriptural teaching, "If any man obey not our word...note that man, and have no company with him that he may be ashamed" (II Thessalonians 3:14).

The Strange Case of Robert Bear

Many people have repented after bearing the weight of the ban in the Reformed Mennonite Church. However, in one strange situation, the shunned person turned on the church with an almost vicious ferocity.

Robert Bear, a Reformed Mennonite farmer from Cumberland County, Pennsylvania, was expelled from the church in 1972 for "railing"—that is vehemently accusing the ministry of dishonesty and disunity. Bear refused to accept the discipline of the church, becoming especially angry when his wife followed the teachings of the church, which require a spouse to withhold marital relations from a shunned partner. Bear took his case to local newspaper and television reporters who were inclined to sympathize with him, primarily, because it was difficult for them to understand the dynamics which led to the church's decision. He also distributed thousands of copies of a vindictive paper called *Reformed Mennonite Times* and published a book on his experiences entitled *Delivered Unto Satan*.

In 1973, Bear decided to take his case to court in an effort to require the church to withdraw the ban. Bear also asked the court to forcibly return his wife and children to his home. However, the Cumberland County Court threw out his case on the grounds of the "free exercise" clause in the first amendment of the U.S. Constitution. In 1975, Bear appealed to the Pennsylvania Supreme Court which insisted that the lower court must first hear the case. Because he had run out of money, Bear decided not to pursue.[5]

But Robert Bear was no quitter. In 1979, he abducted his wife from a local farmers' market. He was arrested and acquitted. In 1983, he showed up at a business establishment owned by his brother-in-law, a Reformed Mennonite bishop. He was towing a gallows behind a pickup truck on which he had hanged a dummy in Mennonite attire. Bear parked in front of the business for three hours and loudly played tape recordings, condemning the shunning practices of the Reformed Mennonites.[6]

Twenty years after his expulsion from the Reformed Mennonites, Robert Bear was still sending out newsletters denouncing his former church's actions and occasionally disrupting Reformed Mennonite Church services. His well known case was actually a highly unusual response to the deeply held Reformed Mennonite belief that the church must be kept pure.

Bishop John Herr officially organized the Reformed Mennonite Church in 1812 near Strasburg, Pennsylvania. However, the group had existed informally from the time of John's father, Frances Herr, who first held separate worship services around 1785.

Growth and Decline of the Reformed Mennonite Church

John Herr spread the Gospel as he understood it with the zeal and persistence of a pioneer circuit rider. His considerable gifts as a speaker and an expositor of the Bible attracted a wide following. Eventually, regular Sunday morning meetings were held in thirteen different places in Lancaster County.[7]

Within John Herr's lifetime, Reformed Mennonite churches were established in Dauphin, Montgomery, Cumberland, and Franklin Counties in Pennsylvania; in Wayne, Fulton, Allen, Clark, and Lucas Counties in Ohio; and at Williamsville, New York and Sterling, Illinois.

Further, Herr's message was also quite well accepted in Canada where six churches had been established by 1850. Herr traveled to many of these widely scattered congregations by horseback. In 1850 while visiting in Humberstone, Ontario, John Herr died at age 68.

The Reformed Mennonite Church continued to grow for a half century after John Herr's death. In 1906, there were 2,079 members[8] in the United States and in 1912 there were 300 members in Canada.[9] The 20th century, however, produced very rapid decline in membership. By 1955, there were only 880 members in the United States and Canada combined.[10]

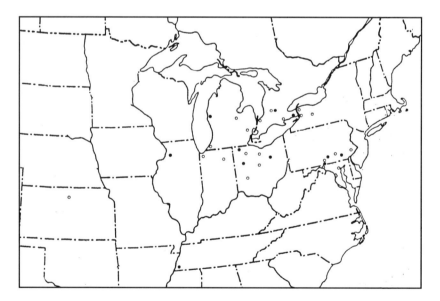

○ *Reformed Mennonite Churches, Extinct*
● *Reformed Mennonite Churches, Present (1996)*

In Lancaster County the thirteen meetingplaces had dwindled to only five by 1965.[11] Some of the meetinghouses were abandoned because use of the automobile made consolidation more practical. And by 1975, there was only one Reformed Mennonite meetinghouse in Lancaster County—Longeneckers, the first and oldest. The decline in membership continues, bringing the total membership down to 412 in 1987[12] and fewer than 400 in 1994. The older people are dying and few young folks are available to take their places.

On the positive side, it should be noted that a few younger people are joining the Reformed Mennonite Church. In 1992, two young men belonging to the Reformed Mennonites graduated from public high school in Lancaster County. In other areas, especially in Canada, congregations appear quite likely to survive indefinitely.

The Reformed Mennonites are careful to say that numbers are not important. They only wish to remain faithful to the Gospel as taught by Menno Simons. As one bishop remarked, "There were only eight on Noah's ark."[13]

The present Longenecker's Reformed Mennonite meetinghouse near Strasburg, Pennsylvania, was built in 1898. The very first Reformed Mennonite meetinghouse was also located on this same site.

The Northeast Hope Reformed Mennonite Church near Kitchener, Ontario, currently has the largest membership (92 in 1987) of any congregation among the Reformed Mennonites.

The Reformed Mennonite Church and Outreach

The Reformed Mennonites have not engaged in organized mission activity, but they have been diligent in spreading the Gospel in their own way. In the 1930s, Bishop Jacob Kreider of Lancaster, Pennsylvania, placed an advertisement in *Sunshine* magazine (a nondenominational religious publication) in which he asked the question, "Does the true Church of Christ exist?" He listed an address for interested persons.

Several people responded, including an African American woman from Memphis, Tennessee, named Lillian Rushing. Kreider sent her literature and began an active correspondence. Rushing, who had become disenchanted with her own church, concluded that the Reformed Mennonites were exactly what she was looking for. Eventually, other members of her family also became interested. The Reformed Mennonite ministry invited the family to become proving members and sent them sets of traditional plain clothing.

Eventually, more than a dozen African Americans in the Memphis area became members of the Reformed Mennonite Church. (They always referred to themselves as "colored," insisting that their color was not black as a hat is "black.") One of the men, Robert Mallory, was ordained as a deacon. Another member, Roosevelt Harris, was a striking figure with his very dark skin and deep blue eyes combined with a plain frock coat and a black hat.

In 1994, there were fewer than ten elderly women who were still members of the Reformed Mennonite Church in Memphis, Tennessee. They were visited monthly by ministers from either Ohio or Illinois. When no minister was present, sermons were read from the prolific writings of the Reformed Mennonites. Unlike other Reformed Mennonite groups, the Memphis group never constructed a meetinghouse, choosing instead to meet in the homes of members.

The Reformed Mennonites were quite open to receiving members from other races and were probably the first Mennonite group to do so. As early as 1840, there were African Americans who had become members of Reformed congregations in Lancaster County, Pennsylvania. One large family even named one of its sons Menno, after Menno Simons.

There was one delicate matter on which the mores of the larger American society had an influence on the church. Reformed

The church at Bluffton, Ohio, is the most active of the three Reformed Mennonite churches in Ohio.

Mennonites have always greeted each other with the holy kiss. Reportedly, the African American members requested that the white members not greet them with the kiss so as not to make trouble for themselves. However, the African-Americans continued to greet each other with the holy kiss.

In the 1960s, this policy was changed when the Civil Rights Movement made the Reformed Mennonites aware of this inconsistency. Today, white and black members greet each other equally with the holy kiss.

Divisions

Despite a strong emphasis on unity, the Reformed Mennonites have experienced two small divisions. The first occurred in 1917 when controversy developed around two issues: 1) conducting funerals in co-operation with ministers who were not Reformed Mennonites; 2) supporting the American Red Cross. Minister John Miller became the leader of the breakaway group, which had three congregations in Ohio. Miller's followers eventually died out and the last church service was held at Willard, Ohio, in 1967. The last member died in 1985.[14]

The second division took place in Lancaster County, Pennsylvania, in 1975 when Minister Willis Weaver and several others were expelled because of their criticism of the Reformed Mennonite leadership. Weaver and his sympathizers organized the United Mennonite Church. This group of fewer than twenty members holds house worship services in several scattered communities.

Distinctive Beliefs

After a prospective member has had a one-year probationary period, Reformed Mennonites administer baptism by pouring, upon confession of faith and evidence of a consistent Christian life. It is quite typical for people raised in the church to put off baptism and church membership until old age. The church teaches that the frivolity and temptations of youth should pass before giving one's life in total commitment to the church.

Reformed Mennonites believe a person becomes a child of God through a radical conversion. This matter is left totally in the hands of God and the Holy Spirit. They maintain that one does not grow into the Christian life. Children and young people in Reformed

Mennonite homes are never pressured into church membership. In fact, teaching children the faith is seen as pointless.

The children of Reformed Mennonites are dressed quite fashionably and are permitted to fully participate in secular society. No Sunday schools or Christian day schools are operated. For example, one woman who became a devout Reformed Mennonite member had been a cheerleader in public high school.

While Reformed Mennonites believe in the necessity of a heartfelt conversion, they do not accept the teaching of assurance of salvation. Like Old Order Mennonites, the Reformed Mennonites hold that one can have hope of salvation but one's eternal destiny is uncertain until arrival at the heavenly gates.

The Reformed Mennonites insist that a member of the church can marry only another church member. Since many members do not affiliate with the church until after marriage, there have been many cases in which one marriage partner belonged to the church and the other did not. Divorce is forbidden for church members, but the Reformed Mennonites are among the few conservative Mennonite groups that accept members who were divorced and remarried, as long as that happened before their conversion to Christian faith.

Like other conservative Mennonites, the Reformed Mennonites believe in non-resistance and do not participate in the military. Neither do they sue at law. Members do not hold public offices nor vote in political elections.

However, unlike other Old Order and Conservative Mennonites, the Reformed Mennonites do not use the lot in selecting their ministers. Election by majority vote has always been the way in which ministers were chosen. Reformed Mennonite ministers have no formal training, but many of the ordained have had a high level of secular education. One current minister attended Yale for a time.

Men and women sit separately in the very plain Reformed Mennonite meetinghouses, but the raised platforms and pulpits so hotly contested by the Old Order Mennonites have been accepted as have public address systems. It is thought that a preacher's table on the same level as the congregation was used at the Longenecker's meetinghouse until a new building was erected in 1898.

The Reformed Mennonites kneel for prayer in their church services, but, unlike Old Order Mennonites, all prayers are audible and spontaneous.

The Reformed Mennonite Home for the aged was built on the west side of the city of Lancaster, Pennsylvania, in 1912. Milton Snavely Hershey, the founder of Hershey Chocolate, endowed a trust fund of $18,000 to the home in memory of his mother, who was a member of the Reformed Mennonites. When the home closed its doors in 1981, the building became an apartment house.

A Famous Son of the Reformed Mennonites

Milton Snavely Hershey (1857-1945), the chocolate king and founder of Hershey Chocolate, was a direct descendent of one of the early Reformed Mennonite bishops, Abraham Snavely (1789-1867). Milton Hershey's mother was a devout member of the Reformed Mennonites. However, Hershey's father never was active in the church, and young Milton followed in his father's footsteps. But throughout his life, he held a deep respect for his mother's faith.

Even after he became very rich and famous, he made a point of attending a Reformed Mennonite church service at least once a year. On these occasions, he would arrive in a chauffeur-driven limousine. His driver would pull up onto the lawn in front of the main entrance of the Reformed Mennonite Church. Milton Hershey would step out of the car, throw down his ever-present cigar, grind it out with his foot, and proceed into the church, where he would sit on the front pew for the service.

He also made an endowment of $18,000 in his mother's memory

to the Reformed Mennonite home for the aged in Lancaster, Pennsylvania, when this institution was built in 1912. (The home was closed in 1981.)

Plain Clothing

Reformed Mennonites adhere to very conservative, uniform plain clothing but have taken a different approach in maintaining this than other conservative Mennonites. They have no actual written or even spoken rules. In their view "love and submission are characteristic of the Christian life; and when these are possessed, there is no contention about dress."[15] It is reasoned that out of love a true follower of Christ will want to appear like the brothers and sisters of the church rather than the unregenerate society.

The earliest members of the Reformed Mennonite Church agreed on a simple style of dress and succeeding generations have seen no need to change. Innovation, it is believed, accommodates fashion and identifies one with the evil world. Consequently, Reformed Mennonite dress styles, especially among the women, have been modified very little over the years. As has already been noted, only baptized members dress in plain clothing. Children and young people dress in the "ways of the world" until the time of their conversion.

Reformed Mennonite Writings

The Reformed Mennonites have always been concerned about letting their "light so shine among men." They have been especially active in the printed ministry. Founder John Herr wrote several small books, including *The True and Blessed Way*. He was also responsible for publishing the first English edition of Menno Simons' *A Foundation* in 1835. It is also possible that Herr was influential in the printing of the first English edition of the *Martyrs' Mirror* in 1836 at Lampeter Square in Lancaster County.

The most well known Reformed Mennonite writer was Daniel Musser (1810-1877), who was not only a bishop in the church but a medical doctor as well. His theological works included *Non-Resistance Asserted* (1864). A copy of this work somehow fell into the hands of Leo Tolstoy and was quoted in Tolstoy's *The Kingdom of God Is Within You*.[16] Daniel Musser's *The Reformed Mennonite Church, Its Rise and Progress, With Its Principles and Doctrines*, published in 1873, was the standard reference on Reformed Mennonites for many years.

Christianity Defined, first published about 1900, was a compilation by Jacob S. Lehman of theological writings by many Reformed Mennonite writers. This is kept in print as an explanation of the group's belief system. The church also distributes a number of tracts and booklets about their faith.

Good Tidings was a monthly magazine published by the Reformed Mennonite Church from 1922 to 1932. Publication was ceased not because of lack of interest but because it was deemed that everything that needed to be said had been said.

The hymnal currently used by the Reformed Mennonites, A *Collection of Hymns*, was compiled in 1910. A section of tunes written in shaped notes appears in the back of this hymnal separate from the hymn texts. The first known hymnal of the church appeared in 1837 and was in German. Ten years later an English hymnal was published which appears to contain only hymns written by Reformed Mennonite authors—a characteristic of all future editions. Hymnals with both English and German sections were issued from 1895 to 1918.[17]

Plain black hats and black bow ties worn with standing collar frock coats are distinguishing characteristics for Reformed Mennonite men. Women of the group wear very conservative plain clothing, including large, distinctive bonnets. Women's clothing is predominately gray in color.

Many of the hymn tunes used by the Reformed Mennonites are familiar to other Christians. They include "What a Friend We Have in Jesus," "Rock of Ages," "Sweet Hour of Prayer," and "Abide With Me." The hymns are sung very slowly and reverently. The song leader sits with the congregation, and the minister who gives out the hymn reads each stanza before it is sung.

The transition from German to English, judging from the publishing record, appears to have started very early and continued over a long period of time. Abraham Brubaker, who retired in 1931, was the last Reformed Mennonite minister in Lancaster County who preached only in German. In Waterloo County, Ontario, the German language was used somewhat later. It is notable that the Reformed Mennonites did not hold as tenaciously to the German language as some other groups, such as the Old Order Mennonites, did. Neither was there ever a controversy over the use of automobiles. Reformed Mennonites purchased and drove automobiles from the earliest years of their common use.

The Conservative Mennonites

6.
The Conservative
Mennonite Conference

The group known today as the Conservative Mennonite Conference is historically much closer to the Amish than to the Mennonites. In the late 1800s most of the Amish who had come to North America divided into two camps—the progressive Amish Mennonites, who eventually merged with the Mennonite Church,

The Conservative Mennonite Conference descends from the Conservative Amish Mennonite Conference which was organized in 1910 by several scattered unaffiliated Amish Mennonite churches. This portrait of the Valentine Bender family, taken about 1910, illustrates the very Amish appearance of the early Conservative Conference members. The Benders were part of the Conservative Amish Mennonite church at Grantsville, Maryland, before they moved to Greenwood, Delaware, in 1914. There they were pioneers in what would become an important Conservative Conference community.

and the more traditional Amish, who came to be called Old Order Amish.

During this time of upheaval, a number of other Amish church districts chose not to identify with either the Old Order Amish or the newly formed Amish Mennonite conferences. These widely scattered Amish congregations wished to accept some innovations adopted by the progressive Amish Mennonites, including Sunday schools, mission involvement, and meetinghouses. Unlike many Amish Mennonites, however, the unaffiliated churches did not want to discard the distinctive plain dress or drop the German language.

In typical Amish manner, these independent churches maintained congregational forms of church government without connections to a wider church structure. During the first decade of the 20th century, however, many felt the need for an organization beyond the local level. In 1910 representatives from three unaffiliated Amish churches met together at Pigeon River, Michigan, for the first Conservative Amish Mennonite Conference.

This group was different from other Amish Mennonite conferences of the time in two significant ways: 1) It was not a regional conference; 2) It was more conservative in its understandings.

By 1920 the number of congregations who identified with the Conservative Conference increased to thirteen. These churches were not interested in creating a centralized, powerful church structure. They merely wanted to create a network through which churches could fellowship and address common concerns. Therefore, the conference did not issue mandates but discussed problems and worked toward consensus among conference participants. The results were usually upheld as appropriate standards.

A Diversity of Churches

Through the years, the churches who identified with the Conservative Amish Mennonite Conference have usually had the same basic ideals and goals, but their backgrounds have often been quite diverse. Some churches have always been independent. Others have come from the more liberal Amish Mennonites. Still others came directly from the deeply traditional Old Order Amish.

The largest community of independent Conservative Amish Mennonite churches was in the Lowville-Croghan area of Lewis County, New York. This community was established by Amish from the Alsace-Lorraine area of France in the 1830s. They fellowshiped with and were closely related to a larger group of Amish who settled in Perth and Waterloo Counties in Ontario about the same time. The Pigeon River Church in Michigan was also independent and was founded by people from Lewis County, New York, who settled in the "thumb" of Michigan in 1900. Pigeon River has always been very active and influential in Conservative Mennonite Conference affairs.

When the Conservative Conference was formed, the Ontario Amish Mennonites were invited to join. They decided against joining because they feared confusing their identity with the Conservative political party in Canada. In 1925, they formed the Ontario Amish Mennonite Conference and, like other regional Amish Mennonite conferences, also eventually affiliated with the Mennonite Church, though not until 1959.

Other Conservative Conference churches such as Townline near Goshen, Indiana, and Locust Grove near Belleville, Pennsylvania, withdrew from the progressive Amish Mennonite movement to identify with the Conservative Conference. Townline was founded in 1876; Locust Grove in 1898. The issues in the Belleville division included continuing use of hooks and eyes, traditional haircuts, four-part singing, and fold-down tops on buggies for the people who became members at Locust Grove.[1] Like the people at Townline,

The Locust Grove Conservative Mennonite Church near Belleville, Pennsylvania, (shown here as it appeared in 1971) began in 1898 as a schism from the more progressive Amish Mennonite churches (now part of the Mennonite Church).

they believed other Amish Mennonites were moving too fast and accepting too many worldly innovations.

Still other Conservative Conference churches came out of traditional Old Order Amish settings. Thus, the Conservatives in Garrett County, Maryland, and Somerset County, Pennsylvania, were actually considered liberals in their own community. In 1895 this border community divided over the issue of shunning those who joined more liberal churches. Those more lenient on this matter sided with Joel J. Miller who was bishop of the Maryland congregation. Those advocating strict avoidance of the excommunicated were under the leadership of Manassas Beachy in Pennsylvania. The Maryland group eventually became part of the Conservative Amish Mennonite Conference while those in Pennsylvania identified with the Old Order Amish.

Conservative Conference people from Garrett County, Maryland, settled near Greenwood, Delaware, in 1914. The Greenwood congregation became one of the largest in the conference and is especially well known because members of this church pioneered the Christian day school movement among Mennonites. The Greenwood Mennonite School was founded in 1927 when students from the Greenwood Church were expelled from public school because of their refusal to salute the American flag.

In 1900 the Amish community around Kalona, Iowa, consisted of four Old Order Amish congregations and two progressive Amish Mennonite congregations. The Old Order churches in the western end of the community—Upper and Lower Deer Creek—followed the Amish Mennonite pattern and built meetinghouses in 1890, gradually moving away from their Old Order Amish identity. Upper Deer Creek affiliated with the Conservative Amish Mennonites in 1915 while Lower Deer Creek joined the progressive Amish Mennonites and merged with the Mennonite Church five years later in 1920.

The Pleasant View Church in Holmes County, Ohio, resulted from a schism with the Old Order Amish in 1912 and affiliated with the Conservative Conference about 1920. The Pleasant View congregation split in 1933, leaving only 21 members in the conference-related group. (The other group became Beachy Amish.) However, ten years later the Conservative Conference Pleasant View Mennonite Church had grown to 200 members. By 1960 Pleasant View had started seven branch congregations with a total membership of nearly 700.

An Amish Influx

The Townline Church in Indiana also experienced a dramatic increase which brought the church from 67 members in 1920 to over 700 in four congregations in 1960.[2] The key to the numerical success at both Townline and Pleasant View appears largely to have resulted from the fact that both congregations were in the center of large Old Order Amish communities. In the first two decades of the 20th century some Old Order Amish were attracted to the Conservative Conference because of its emphasis on both traditional non-conformity and evangelicalism.

After 1920 the Conservatives had an even stronger drawing card—the automobile. As cars became accessible to rural people and as the Old Order Amish continued to say no to this innovation, some Amish looked for a church where they "could have their cake and eat it too." Those Amish who wished to retain an emphasis on traditional values and yet embrace modern technology and evangelicalism found the Conservative Conference a welcome haven. It is said that many Old Order Amish "went liberal and joined the Conservatives."

Conservative Amish Mennonite congregations consisting of former Old Order Amish were also established in a number of other communities—Plain City, Ohio, in 1938; Arthur, Illinois, in 1945; Hutchinson, Kansas, and Geauga County, Ohio, in 1947; Dover, Delaware, in 1954; and Nappanee, Indiana, in 1955.

Be Not Conformed

The churches which affiliated with the Conservative Amish Mennonite Conference in the early 1900s were decidedly more traditional in dress standards than the regional Amish Mennonite conferences which eventually merged with the Mennonite Church. However, there was also considerable variation in practice within the Conservative Conference itself. Some churches required the plain coat with standing collar. Some insisted on hooks and eyes; others permitted buttons. Conventional coats worn without a necktie were the norm in many churches. Many men wore short, trimmed beards, but few congregations actually required this after about 1920. Women's dress was less diverse in the early years but many differences developed later.

Surprisingly, the German language decreased in importance

among the Conservative Amish Mennonites very soon after the group organized. For the first nine years, all conference proceedings were conducted in German. In 1919, the minutes appeared in both German and English, and beginning in 1923, the conference minutes were published only in English. In 1928 several speakers were assigned English topics for the first time at the Conference gathering.[3] The Conservative Conference cooperated with Old Order Amish and later Beachy Amish in producing the German-English *Herold der Wahrheit* until 1955. About this time the last Conservative Conference congregation to use German switched to all English services.

Missions

From the very beginning, Conservative Amish Mennonite Conference congregations have had a keen interest in missions. The first mission endeavor was the Amish Mennonite Children's Home established at Accident, Maryland, in 1914. This institution thrived until 1938 when it closed its doors. Other mission opportunities were developing for Conservative Conference congregations.

The mission board of the conference, established in 1919, explored many possibilities for home missions—both rural and urban. The first project was a city mission at Flint, Michigan, in 1929. From 1946 to 1950 several missions were started in eastern Kentucky's Appalachia. In 1950 the Conference took over the relief work begun by Mennonite Central Committee at Espelkamp, Germany. In 1951 they established a mission in Luxembourg. Missionaries were sent to Costa Rica in 1962, Nicaragua in 1968, and Ecuador in 1980.

The Central American churches resulting from these missions organized independent conferences in the 1970s but have continued to maintain close ties with the Conservative Conference. The mission board set up headquarters at Rosedale, Ohio, in 1973 and became Rosedale Mennonite Missions.

Rosedale Bible Institute

A very important part of the program of the Conservative Conference began at the Pleasant View meetinghouse near Berlin, Ohio, in 1952. A Conservative Amish Mennonite Bible School was founded. This conference-supported school replaced a number of congregational and community Bible schools which had operated at

The Conservative Amish Mennonite Conference became the Conservative Mennonite Conference in 1954. This photograph of the students and faculty of Berlin Bible School (now Rosedale Bible Institute) was taken that same year.

various Conservative Amish Mennonites congregations as early as the 1920s.

The immediate success of the school soon taxed the facilities at Pleasant View. In fact the church was so dominated by Bible School students that many members felt crowded out and attended other churches while the school was in session for six weeks each winter. Eleven years later in 1963, the institution moved to a former public school building at Rosedale, Ohio. Reflecting the higher level of education offered at the school, the name became Rosedale Bible Institute in 1971.

Movement Toward the Mennonite Church

Through the years the Conservative Amish Mennonites drew closer and closer to the Mennonite Church. Representatives were sent to the General Council of the Mennonite Church's General Conference, beginning in 1950. Within the decade of the 1950s, representatives were also appointed to the publication board of the Mennonite Church, the Mennonite Board of Education and the Eastern Mennonite College (now University) consultative council.

BERLIN BIBLE SCHOOL 1954

This identification with the Mennonite Church brought along with it a distancing from the Amish roots of the Conservative Conference. In 1954 the name was changed from Conservative Amish Mennonite Conference to Conservative Mennonite Conference. By the time of the name change, there was little Amish influence evident in the Conservative Conference. Hooks and eyes on men's coats and the wearing of beards were rare. Few congregations still insisted on solid colored fabric for clothing. The last churches to use German in their services were giving it up. By the late 1950s and 1960s, the Conservative Conference was more like the larger Mennonite Church, and, like that body, had both liberal and conservative elements within its ranks.

By this time, the Mennonite Church had reached the peak of a conservative-traditional-fundamentalist emphasis and was beginning to move toward modernization. Many Conservative Conference members also began moving in that direction.

However, some Conservatives were soon expressing great concern about worldly trends developing in the conference. These included the use of television and the wearing of wedding bands, as well as a trend for men to wear neckties and women to cut their hair and drop the traditional head coverings. A group presented a paper to the 1967 conference asking that discipline be increased in these areas. A special committee was assigned to study the matters, but

This 1969 wedding scene at the United Bethel Conservative Mennonite Church at Plain City, Ohio, illustrates the style of dress then prevalent. (Several women in the photo are Beachy Amish.) Some Conservative Conference churches still hold to more conservative standards than the conference in general.

no strong actions were taken to restore the old standards.

When the Conservative Mennonite Bible School at Berlin, Ohio, was founded in 1952, the dress standards of the Conservative Amish Mennonite Conference were rigidly upheld. This included a ban on neckties, and the requirement that women wear a head covering and have their hair pinned up. But, as the majority of conference churches changed their standards and as the school attracted an increasingly higher number of students from more modern groups, the school, by then called Rosedale Bible Institute, felt compelled to change its personal appearance requirements. In 1985, Rosedale insisted only that students abide by the dress standards of their individual congregations.[4]

The Conservative Conservatives

To avoid this drift toward the world, some individuals and occasionally entire congregations began withdrawing from the Conservative Mennonite Conference in the late 1950s. However, some traditional Conservatives also stayed in the conference. In 1994 a remnant of congregations continued to uphold at least some of the old standards. These churches recognized each other in an informal way and associated somewhat with churches in the Conservative Mennonite Movement (see chapter 8). Conservative Conference members are some of the most active participants in the Fellowship of Concerned Mennonites and the Evangelical Anabaptist Fellowship, two concern groups working within mainstream Mennonite groups.

The Rosedale Bible Institute has been one of the most important Conservative Conference institutions. The headquarters of the Conference and the mission board office (Rosedale Mennonite Missions) are also located in the small village of Rosedale near Columbus, Ohio.

The Pleasant Grove Conservative Mennonite Church near Goshen, Indiana (top), and the United Bethel Conservative Mennonite Church of Plain City, Ohio (bottom), are two congregations in the Conservative Mennonite Conference which have tried to maintain traditional standards on non-conformity to the world.

Movement Away from the Mennonite Church

Because the Conservative Mennonite Conference is more inclined toward fundamentalism than the Mennonite Church General Assembly, they began expressing considerable wariness of the Mennonite Church's theologically liberal tendencies early in the 1990s. In 1991, the Conservative Conference issued the Conservative Mennonite Statement of Theology which affirms their strong biblical faith. The inspiration and inerrancy of the Bible are supported. Evolution is rejected. Women are not permitted in pastoral leadership positions. In 1994, a minister was dismissed

Contemporary styles of worship and traditional Mennonite symbols both find expression at the Conservative Mennonite Conference annual meeting in 1993, held in Goshen, Indiana.

because of his tolerance of homosexuality. It was decided that all ministers in the Conservative Mennonite Conference must sign a paper, affirming their agreement with this statement on theology.

Then after years of what appeared to be imminent amalgamation with the Mennonite Church General Assembly, the Conservative Conference made a dramatic shift away from that group. As recently as 1972, the Conservatives had declined full participation in the General Assembly. In 1992, an official statement was made by the Conservative Conference declaring its stance as being "an autonomous circle of fellowship within the worldwide Mennonite church." The statement goes on to say, "We will continue to pursue decisions about relationships with other circles of fellowship as we sense the Lord's leading. This means that the Conservative Mennonite Conference shall move ahead positively with autonomy in theology, organization, identity, polity, and activity, with a readiness to interact from that base with other groups in ways consistent with the CMC position in the above named categories."[5]

In 1993 after having had an official member on the General Board of the Mennonite Church for a decade, the Conservative Conference

The Conservative Conference has been very active in missions, especially in Latin America. The Spanish-speaking Mennonite pastor at left ministers at a mission in San Antonio, Texas. Missions begun by the Conservative Conference in Costa Rica and Honduras developed into separate conferences.

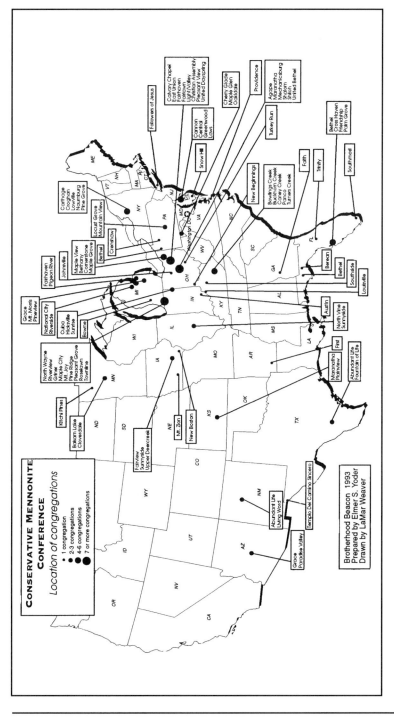

Conservative Mennonite Conference Churches

135

reverted to sending a representative as a non-voting observer only. And in 1995, the Conservative Mennonite Conference asked to be listed in a separate section of the *Mennonite Yearbook* to make it clear that they were an autonomous group and not a conference of the Mennonite Church General Assembly.

By this time, the Conservative Mennonite Conference bore little outward resemblance to the group that first met in 1910. The lot is seldom used to select ministers. Full-time pastors are fully supported by many churches. In most congregations, plain coats, cape dresses, and covering strings are gone. Instead one finds instrumental music, neckties, wedding rings, and women with short hair. In an increasing number of churches, coverings have even become scarce.

However, Conservative Conference congregations still stand firmly on non-resistance and continue to practice feet washing consistently. While most congregations will accept members who have been divorced and remarried before conversion, the church is officially opposed to ministers performing marriages for those who have been divorced. As has been noted, the Conservative Mennonite Conference remains quite conservative in its theology.

7.
Blending the New and the Old

The Mennonite Church underwent rapid, extensive change during the last quarter of the 19th century, but a core of traditional beliefs and practices were retained into the beginning of the 20th century. Members of the Mennonite Church were still "Plain People." In some ways, they were committed to the biblical principle of non-conformity to the world with greater zeal than they had been during earlier years of their history. Distinctive plain dress was actively promoted and all jewelry, including wedding bands, was forbidden. The practices of feet washing, the holy kiss, and the head covering for women were taught as ordinances of the church equal to baptism and communion.

True to their Anabaptist heritage, members of the Mennonite Church strongly upheld believers' baptism and non-resistance. The leadership of the church—bishops, ministers, and deacons—was still selected by lot from the congregation. Leaders received no salary.

During those years, the Mennonite Church often succeeded in blending the ways of evangelical Protestantism with distinctive traditional practices. While lively gospel songs largely replaced the traditional hymns which had been sung to slow tunes, all congregational singing was still unaccompanied. In the large Lancaster County, Pennsylvania, Mennonite community the old-style preachers' table gave way to the pulpit on a raised platform, but men and women continued to sit in separate sections.

While most leaders in the Mennonite Church valued their distinctive beliefs and practices, they felt it was imperative to intro-

The traditional Mennonite practices of separate seating for men and women, a cappella singing, plain clothing, plural ministry, and simple meetinghouse architecture were very much in evidence at the Deep Run (Franconia Conference) Mennonite Church in 1938 when this picture was taken.

duce new methods to preserve these essentials of the faith. They sought to make the church more accessible and appealing to the youth and to the outside world. To accomplish this goal, church services were conducted in English rather than the traditional German, Sunday schools were introduced to instruct young people in scriptural truths, and revival meetings were instituted to draw the unconverted into the church. To indoctrinate older youth, Bible schools and colleges were established. Church periodicals were founded to provide wholesome, doctrinally sound reading for church families. A new sense of responsibility to the unconverted masses developed, and mission programs were organized to carry the gospel to the spiritually deprived both in North American cities and in foreign countries. All of these programs led to a plethora of institutions.

Strong Leaders and Firm Convictions

These new institutions ultimately became the most powerful forces in the life of the church, and their leaders wielded increasing influence. John F. Funk and John S. Coffman, as founders of some of the first Mennonite institutions, became the most influential people in the early part of this new era in the Mennonite Church. Coffman died in 1899 and the prestige of John F. Funk waned in the early 1900s. Daniel Kauffman (1865-1944), a school teacher from Missouri who was converted at a John S. Coffman revival meeting, became the next prime shaper of life and thought in the Mennonite Church. Kauffman was ordained a preacher in 1892 and bishop in 1896.

In 1905 he became founding editor of *The Gospel Witness* to rival John F. Funk's *Herald of Truth*. However, by 1908 the two publications had merged to become The *Gospel Herald*, edited by Daniel Kauffman. *Gospel Herald* is still the official weekly magazine of the Mennonite Church. While Kauffman continued Funk's and Coffman's fervent emphasis on evangelism and revivalism, he went further than either of these leaders in articulating and strengthening distinctive Mennonite beliefs and practices.

Kauffman exerted considerable influence on the church during his 38 years as a church periodical editor. He also formulated a doctrinal manual in 1898 which went through several editions and was regarded as the official expression of Mennonite Church theology for many years. Perhaps the most significant contribution Daniel Kauffman made to the Mennonite Church was the key role he played in organizing the Mennonite Church General Conference (now called the General Assembly) in 1898, bringing scattered regional conferences into a working relationship with each other.

Daniel Kauffman and other leaders of his time saw a need to clearly define Mennonite doctrine and practice. To avoid ambiguity and safeguard against apostasy and worldliness, detailed doctrinal statements were formulated and very specific standards of conduct were enacted. Adherence to the established order became mandatory for members of the Mennonite Church. A centralized form of church government developed to uphold the doctrines and practices and to keep order within the church. The ordained men were given the responsibility to maintain discipline in the local churches; the regional conferences had control over the churches under their jurisdictions; and the General Conference was given authority over the regional conferences.

Daniel Kauffman (1865-1944); shown with his typewriter ca.1913 (top), with his wife Mary in Scottdale, Pennsylvania, in 1933 (bottom), and sitting at his desk (facing page); exerted a strong conservative influence on the Mennonite Church as a bishop, author, periodical editor, and organizer.

The Prerogative of Plainness

While John Funk and John Coffman encouraged distinctive plain dress for Mennonites in the 1880s and 1890s, Daniel Kauffman and his associates went a step further. They worked at making plainness compulsory for all members of the Mennonite Church. Kauffman and other revivalists saw the need to bring about uniformity and consistency in the matter of dress. Also because the Mennonite Church felt the call to minister to those outside their fold, a Christian uniform was seen as an aid to witnessing to sinful society.

What became known as the regulation garb for men consisted of a plain-crowned black hat and a coat buttoning to the neck with a narrow standing collar and no lapels. In obedience to the teachings of I Corinthians 11, women wore a plain, cap-type covering made of white net material over their pinned up long hair. When going out-

The regulation plain dress of the Mennonite Church is clearly illustrated in this photo of the first graduating class of Eastern Mennonite School (now called Eastern Mennonite University) in 1919. Standard dress for men included standing collar, plain suitcoats worn without neckties. Standard dress for women included unadorned cape dresses, head coverings with tie strings, and uncut hair parted in the center. Many conservative Mennonites in the 1990s continue to dress much as these Mennonite Church folks did in 1919.

doors, a black bonnet was to be worn over the covering. The pre-scribed style for dresses was free of ornamentation and had a ker-chief-like cape over the bodice and was worn with an apron.

This basic style of clothing was not invented by the turn-of-the-century revivalists, as some historians have implied. Rather, the forms the revivalists promoted were drawn from an older tradition. Many photographs from the mid 1800s—before the revivalist move-ment—show older Mennonite people wearing the same basic tradi-tional garb later encouraged by the revivalists.

Furthermore, the Reformed Mennonites, who originated in the 1780s, and the Stauffer Mennonites, who broke with the main body of the Mennonite Church in 1845, insisted on uniform plain dress which looks quite similar to the regulation dress encouraged by Kauffman and others in the early 1900s. No doubt, the Reformed and Stauffer styles were representative of the most conservative Mennonite standards at the time of their respective breaks with the larger church.

In the early 1900s, many members of the Mennonite Church did not believe the fads and fancies of worldly fashion should dictate what they wore. They considered it important to establish a stan-dard of dress based on Christian principles. As fashionable styles for women became more extreme and further removed from tradi-tional standards of decency and modesty in the 1920s, the need to make a clear distinction between the church and the world became increasingly more obvious.

From about 1910 to 1950, a large percentage of Mennonite Church members wore some form of distinctive dress. However, the cam-paign to establish a uniform standard of dress throughout the church was not entirely successful. Some generalities developed.

For example, during the first half of the 20th century, plain cloth-ing was more common and lasted longer in the eastern United States than in the Midwest and the West. It was more consistently worn by women than men and was stressed more for the ordained than lay members. Throughout most of the Mennonite Church in the 1940s, women wore white net head coverings, did not cut their hair, and did not wear makeup or jewelry. Neither sex wore wedding bands. Ordained men were expected to wear the regulation plain coat. Some more conservative congregations required all members to wear complete regulation garb.

Jacob and Elizabeth Rosenberger (above) of the Franconia Mennonite Conference posed for this picture circa 1880. Jacob wears an early form of the traditional standing collar plain coat. Elizabeth appears in the cap, cape, and apron typical of conservative Mennonite women of the time. Their clothing is clearly different than the prevailing styles of the day. About twenty years later in 1901, Benjamin F. and Lizzie Hershey Denlinger (facing page) of Lancaster County, Pennsylvania, posed for their wedding photo. Their clothing is very similar to the earlier style of plain clothing worn by the Rosenbergers. Later Mennonite men further simplified their clothing by not wearing ties.

Eastern Mennonite School, Harrisonburg, Virginia, was established in 1917 as a conservative alternative to Goshen College in Indiana. Here John L. Stauffer and Amos D. Wenger, both staunch conservative thinkers, preside over the plainly dressed student body about 1930. Fifty years later there were few vestiges of outward Mennonite symbols to be seen at the school.

Right Doctrine

Mennonites were not only concerned about matters of outward piety but focused equal attention on inner faith. As the fundamentalist-modernist debate broiled in American Protestantism in the 1910s and 1920s, an intense anti-modernist campaign was launched in the Mennonite Church. At the 1921 Mennonite General Conference at Garden City, Missouri, an official doctrinal statement called *Christian Fundamentals* was adopted.

This new confession of faith consisted of eighteen articles affirming the fundamentals of the Mennonite faith. On the matters of the inspiration of the Bible, the authenticity of the Genesis account of creation, the deity of Jesus Christ, salvation by grace through faith, the work of the Holy Spirit, and the assurance of salvation, the Mennonite doctrinal statement was in basic agreement with fundamentalist Protestants. Differing from most other theologically conservative Christian groups, the Mennonite Church further included in its basic beliefs separation from the world, the exercise of discipline in the church, and the ordinances of feetwashing, the prayer covering, the holy kiss, and anointing with oil. The 1921 *Confession of Faith* also specified the wearing of modest apparel, forbad swearing of oaths, prohibited membership in secret orders, and banned life insurance. In its most radical departure from the larger fundamentalist movement, the Mennonite Church also held to separation of church and state and refused to take part in warfare.

John Horsch (1867-1941) championed doctrinal orthodoxy and conservative Mennonite thought and practice through his prolific writings. This portrait, probably taken at the time the German-born couple was married in 1893, shows that Christine (Funck) Horsch had not yet conformed completely to American Mennonite dress standards while John appears in very conservative plain dress.

In addition to the 1921 *Confession of Faith*, the 1898 Manual of Bible Doctrine by Daniel Kauffman—with its subsequent editions, *Bible Doctrine* (1914) and *Doctrines of the Bible* (1928)—further established an orthodox set of beliefs and practices. Kauffman wrote a number of other books and tracts defending the faith. He was aided by the prolific writings of John Horsch (1867-1941), a well educated German immigrant employed by the Mennonite Publishing House, who forthrightly exposed what he saw as the errors of the liberal Mennonites of the time.

The modern ideas attacked by Kauffman and Horsch primarily originated and disseminated from Goshen College, the first institution of higher learning in the Mennonite Church. At the height of the controversy, Goshen College was closed for the 1923-24 school year. It reopened with a new faculty more sympathetic to the accepted church order.

Many of the liberal thinkers implicated in the struggle transferred to the General Conference Mennonite Church (not to be confused with the Mennonite Church General Conference), including several Goshen College faculty members who became professors at colleges affiliated with the more liberal General Conference Mennonite Church.

Dealing with Deviance

The 1930s and early 1940s marked the time in recent history when the Mennonite Church leadership had its most thorough commitment to conservative theology and traditional non-conformity to the world. There were many members, however, who resented and resisted the prescribed dress standards and other church rules. In some areas those who chose not to follow the regulations were not disciplined according to the directives of the conference.

At a special session of the General Conference (later called the General Assembly) of the Mennonite Church in 1944, a proposal was made to disfellowship any regional conference that did not enforce the official dress standards. While this recommendation had the support of many of the delegates, it failed to pass.[1]

The year 1944 marked the end of an era with the death of Daniel Kauffman. While the patterns he helped set became the standard for conservative Mennonitism for virtually the entire 20th century, many of Kauffman's ideals came under question soon after his pass-

George R. Brunk I *founded the* Sword and Trumpet *magazine in 1929 as an ultra-conservative voice in the Mennonite Church. The publication continues today and is edited by his son, George* R. Brunk II.

The Sword and Trumpet *has always spoken boldly against modern trends in the Mennonite Church. Already in 1930 a cartoonist for the magazine, Ernest Gehman, depicted Mennonite distinctives (top) being seriously undermined by those within their gates. The second cartoon (bottom) drawn by Gehman in 1931 warned of the evils of radio.*

ing. The new leadership was less committed to traditional non-conformity than Kauffman's generation had been.

New Leaders, Different Directions

In the post World War II period, two men became particularly influential as leaders in the Mennonite Church. They were Harold S. Bender (1897-1962) and Orie O. Miller (1892-1977). Both men were highly involved in many of the institutions and agencies of the church. Bender was primarily an educator at Goshen College and a renowned church historian.

In 1944 Bender wrote *The Anabaptist Vision* which reinterpreted the beginnings of the Mennonite Church and gave a new generation inspiration and an appreciation for its heritage. Miller was instrumental in founding the Mennonite Central Committee (MCC), an international relief agency which he led for many years. The emphasis on peace and service which developed in the Mennonite Church was largely due to the efforts of Orie Miller and MCC.

Neither Bender nor Miller were ordained preachers, as most earlier church leaders had been. Bender was ordained only after he became the first dean of Goshen College Biblical Seminary in 1944. He never pastored a church. Both men graduated from Goshen College during its pre-1920s liberal era. While Bender and Miller submitted to the dress standards of the Mennonite Church by wearing the regulation plain coat, neither actively promoted traditional garb. Both men took a moderate position on theological issues, being neither openly liberal nor conservative.

Bender and Miller were typical of the new set of leaders coming into power in the mid 1940s. The transition from a church administered by unsalaried, self-educated ministers to a highly bureaucratic church organization run by college-educated intellectuals and professionals was nearly complete in the Mennonite Church by the 1950s. The professionally trained preachers produced by Goshen College Biblical Seminary began replacing the lay ministers ordained by lot in many congregations. Some of the older traditional ministers felt intimidated by the more articulate progressives and kept silent as radical changes were instituted in the churches and the denomination.

The involvement of the Mennonite Church in the Civilian Public Service program for conscientious objectors during World War II fur-

After World War II the leadership of the Mennonite Church became increasingly dominated by college-educated professionals who passively ascribed to outward distinctives to keep peace with the conservatives but did not actively promote traditional non-conformity. The Mennonite Relief Committee shown here in 1952 includes some of the most influential men in the church. Harold S. Bender is standing second from the left. Orie O. Miller is seated on the far right.

ther exposed it to influences from more liberal church groups. Many young men, isolated from their home churches and communities in CPS camps, were persuaded to abandon the plain life either by exposure to secular society or other religious groups. As the need for post-war relief work presented itself, many Mennonites saw the doctrine of non-conformity to the world as a hindrance in their efforts to serve the world.

Plain Becomes Passé

Soon after World War II, open criticism of traditional beliefs and practices began to be seen and heard in the Mennonite Church. In October 1950, *Gospel Herald* published the articles "What Basis Nonconformity?" by Daniel Hertzler (who later became the editor of the magazine) and "What's Wrong with Nonconformity?" by Richard Burkholder (who later was a professor at Goshen College). Both articles were originally orations given at Eastern Mennonite College.[2]

As an observer of the 1953 session of the Mennonite Church General Conference the editor of *Sword and Trumpet* noted, "Unless appearances are deceptive in a gathering of this sort, we are rapidly leaving our conservative patterns of attire. Any kind of fashion is greatly in evidence. Much bobbed hair may be seen. Many ministers are wearing neckties, and the Ministerial Committee, as shown by its report, is entertaining the matter of the validity of the plain coat as a requirement for ministers."[3]

By 1959 the scene at General Conference had become even more lamentable to another editor of The Sword and Trumpet. "Much carelessness in evidence on matters of attire, showing that the Church has reached a dangerous permissive stage on this question. Some men in thin, short-sleeved sport shirts. Many local women in sleeveless, low-cut dresses contrasting sharply with plain folk from the 'provinces.' Much cut hair in evidence on the part of women in modern coiffure, some times topped by a small devotional covering, but most often not. Not a word of concern for such matters in this conference. Perhaps General Conference leaves such things to the district conferences, and the district conferences leave it to the people, and the people follow what they see on their TV sets."[4]

When this meeting of the General Conference (now called General Assembly) of the Mennonite Church was held at Kalona, Iowa, in 1941, dress standards related to non-conformity to the world were still very much in effect.

Mennonites and the Media

The matter of non-conformity in dress was the subject most often attacked and neglected in the mid-century Mennonite Church. However, other areas of separation from the world were also eroding. Traditional attitudes toward entertainment were rapidly changing. When radios became available in the 1920s, the Mennonite Church took a strong stand against them. Eventually radios gained acceptance in many areas and some Mennonites saw an opportunity to send the gospel message across the airwaves. The Calvary Hour was begun by a Mennonite minister in Ohio in 1936, but the broadcast was not widely accepted in the church. In 1951 the Mennonite Hour radio program began at Harrisonburg, Virginia. By 1953 it was officially supported by the Mennonite Board of Missions and Charities.

Television became the next center of controversy. Like many other conservative Christian groups, the Mennonite Church immediately saw that television would bring many harmful influences into the homes of members. The Lancaster Mennonite Conference for-

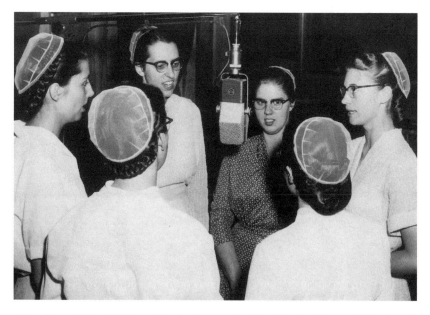

Once the majority of Mennonites had accepted radio, the church entered the broadcasting world with the Mennonite Hour *in 1951. These women singers, ca.1960, demonstrate the mixture of plain and more fashionable dress typical of that time.*

bad its members to own televisions in 1943 when the devices were still only in the developmental stage. The same conference ruled in 1949, "Brethren or sisters who are responsible for the sale and or use of television forfeit their membership."[5] Other conferences were not as severe in their pronouncements against what some called "the evil box," and even in the Lancaster Conference members clandestinely watched television in attics and basements until official prohibition was widely lifted in the 1960s.

For the first half of the 20th century the Mennonite Church forbad attendance at movies, live dramas, and other amusements that were considered frivolous, if not harmful, entertainment. Again, restrictions were eased in the 1960s and Mennonites not only began attending theaters, but also began putting on productions of their own. Resistance to social dancing lasted a bit longer, but Mennonite colleges allowed dances on their campuses in the 1980s after having winked at off-campus dances for years. Liturgical dance presentations became part of church conference programs in the 1970s.

Participation in team sports on anything beyond a very informal level was strongly discouraged during the first half of the 20th century. The Mennonite Board of Education had prohibited inter-school sports activities in 1920. After much controversy, intercollegiate sports competition was approved at Goshen College in 1956. The trend soon spread to other Mennonite Church colleges and high schools.

Musical instruments made their appearance in the homes of Mennonite Church members quite early in the 20th century. Some rather conservative church leaders had pianos or organs in their homes but were adamantly opposed to installing these instruments in churches. In the 1960s a few congregations in the Mennonite Church began using piano or organ music for preludes, offertories, special singing, and weddings. Many churches eventually began instrumental accompaniment of congregational singing.

Mennonites and the New Morality

In the last years of the 20th century, many Mennonites not only became outwardly assimilated into American society, but also yielded to pressures to compromise some of their basic moral standards. For example, the Mennonite Church was very much opposed to divorce. They interpreted Christ's teaching to mean that the innocent victim of a divorce could not remarry as long as a former spouse was still living. This position became increasingly difficult to uphold as mission work brought in people who were divorced and remarried, and the marriages of more and more children of the church began breaking up.

Most regional conferences of the Mennonite Church eventually reinterpreted their position and began accepting members who had been divorced and remarried before experiencing conversion. Individual congregations were ultimately given the responsibility of determining membership standards regarding marital relationships. Many have consequently accepted members who have been married, divorced, and remarried even within the church.

The Choice to Change

A major turning point in the Mennonite Church came at the General Conference of 1963 held in Kalona, Iowa. The theme of this meeting was change and the church was indeed in the midst of a period of radical change. At this gathering a new *Mennonite Confession of Faith* replaced the 1921 doctrinal statement. In addition, plans for a massive reorganization were initiated at the 1963 conference, culminating at the 1971 Mennonite Church General Assembly at Kitchener, Ontario.

Among the many structural changes which went into effect was the renaming of the biennial gathering from Mennonite Church General Conference to Mennonite Church General Assembly, to distinguish the group from the General Conference Mennonite Church. Lay delegates were invited to participate in the new General Assembly, whereas only ordained men had taken part in the General Conference. Former committees and boards merged into five commissions. The role of the bishop was redefined or eliminated, and a shift from conference to congregational decision making was suggested. Women could now be delegates in the General Assembly, and some conferences began ordaining women to the ministry.

The Mennonite Church did not escape the restlessness and questioning of authority that typified the 1960s. Many Mennonites saw the restrictions the church placed on them as a form of bondage and pressed for radical change. A trend to replace the emphasis on non-conformity to the world with service to the physical needs of the world developed. There was also a shift from non-resistance to peace activism. Mennonite youth joined the peace movement in actively protesting the Vietnam War. There was also increased Mennonite participation in the Civil Rights movement and other efforts concerned with social injustice. Many Mennonites felt a responsibility to witness to the state, resulting in increased involvement with politics.

Communion was held at General Conference for the first time in 1967. This was the beginning of open communion in the Mennonite Church. Before this time, churches had generally conducted council meetings prior to communion services. These meetings generally stressed that all members should be in unity with the church and should live according to the discipline.

A major indication of the shift in emphasis for the Mennonite Church was the 1995 decision to work toward a merger with the General Conference Mennonite Church, once considered a wayward, liberal cousin.

The theme of the 1993 session of the Mennonite Church General Assembly was indicative of the liberation many members felt.

The Conservative Cry

As the Mennonite Church moved away from conservatism in lifestyle and doctrine in the late 20th century, a significant minority were unwilling to follow in what they perceived to be a "broad path to destruction." Many of these dissenters tried to halt the progress of liberalism through preaching, the founding of periodicals and publishing houses, and the formation of concern groups. Because the rapid advance of modernism could not be curbed in the Mennonite Church, most of the conservative groups and individuals withdrew and organized independent Mennonite groups.

This late 20th century phenomenon might be called the Conservative Mennonite Movement. It is quite separate from the Conservative Mennonite Conference which originated much earlier. Today, most of these independent conservative Mennonite groups consider the Conservative Conference much too liberal and have no fellowship with Conservative Conference congregations. However, many of the most conservative members of the Conservative Conference have withdrawn their affiliation with that Conference and have formed congregations which are part of the Conservative Mennonite Movement.

8.
The Growing
Conservative Mennonite
Movement

A movement emerged after World War II in reaction to the liberal trends within the Mennonite Church. Like the Old Order movement in the 19th century, the 20th century Conservative Mennonite Movement developed from scattered separatist groups which arose sporadically over a long period of time. Many of the individual groups began as reform movements within the Mennonite Church. Most eventually withdrew their affiliation with regional conferences when their efforts to stop the influx of progressive ideas proved futile.

The first of these conservative withdrawals from the Mennonite Church occurred in the 1950s, and they continue in the 1990s. Many independent single congregations developed from this exodus. These groups choose independence primarily because they remain suspicious of a monolithic church structure. Many of these Mennonites believe that a large, complex, bureaucratic church structure was part of the downfall of the Mennonite Church. Some parts of the movement have been known as Non-Conference Mennonites or Non-Conference Conservatives because of their antipathy to the Conference structure.

By the 1970s the Conservative Mennonite Movement was firmly established. Several well organized groups cooperated with each other in many common concerns. All the groups are in general agreement on the fundamental conservative Mennonite practices such as women's head coverings, distinctive plain dress, a cappella congregational singing, no use of television, and no tolerance for divorce

"Taking water"

and remarriage. However, as time went on, it became apparent that there were many differences of opinion on various other issues between and within the various groups. Details on dress standards, permissible youth activities, use of the radio, musical instruments in the home, and forms of church government were some of the main points of controversy. Eventually, many of the groups within the Conservative Mennonite Movement divided rather than continue in disunity. The Conservative Mennonite Movement eventually polarized into several indistinct circles of fellowship.

Today, there is some overlapping of these circles. Further, some groups do not fit neatly into any classification. Although there are no official names for these groupings, they can be divided into five categories: ultra-conservative, intermediate-conservative, moderate-conservative, fundamental-conservative, and theological-conservative.

The ultra-conservatives maintain very detailed standards of dress

"Now what?"

These cartoons, (above and facing page) which appeared in two consecutive 1973 issues of Life Lines of the Southeastern Mennonite Conference, graphically illustrate how those in the Conservative Mennonite Movement view their relationship to each other and to the Mennonite Church.

and behavior. The final authority of the ordained men in church matters is recognized. Youth activities are very limited. These groups are adamantly opposed to the use of radios and have little or no fellowship with other groups in the Conservative Mennonite Movement who do tolerate radios. All of the ultra-conservative groups use Sunday school materials from Rod and Staff Publishers.

While the moderate-conservatives abide by the same general rules as the ultra-conservatives, they are not quite as precise in their expectations. For example, shoes and stockings other than black are permitted in many of these congregations and groups. In most cases, members of moderate congregations have more of a voice in the affairs of the church. Youth are permitted to have their own activities. While most of the moderate groups strongly discourage the

TABLE SEVEN

Membership in
Conservative Mennonite Groups

	churches	*members*
Ultra-Conservatives		
Conservative Mennonite Fellowship	7	279
Nationwide Mennonite Fellowship[1]	66	2,546
Conservative Mennonite Churches of Ontario	9	347
Washington-Franklin Mennonite Conference	12	1,126
Eastern Pennsylvania Mennonite Church	59	3,434
York-Adams Conservative Mennonite Churches	5	238
Ohio Wisler Mennonite Churches[2]	4	350 est.
	Total	**8,320**
Intermediate-Conservatives		
Western Conservative Mennonite Fellowship	11	451
Bethel Conservative Fellowship	8	355
Pilgrim Mennonite Conference	12	772
Unaffiliated Conservative Mennonite Churches[3]	4	222
	Total	**1,800**
Moderate-Conservatives		
Cumberland Valley Mennonite Church	6	410
Mid-Atlantic Mennonite Fellowship	13	1,072
Southeastern Mennonite Conference	14	770
South Atlantic Mennonite Conference	3	189
Mid-West Mennonite Fellowship	34	1,892
Hope Mennonite Fellowship	4	274
Southern Mennonite Fellowship[4]	11	655
Unaffiliated Conservative Mennonite Churches[3]	19	1,359
	Total	**6,621**
Fundamental-Conservatives		
Bible Mennonite Fellowship[5]	6	774
Sharing Concerns Mennonite Bible Conference	8	584
Keystone Mennonite Fellowship[6]	28	1,978
Unaffiliated Conservative Mennonite Churches[3]	11	623
	Total	**3,959**
Total of all of the above	**354**	**20,700**

Theological-Conservatives		
Conservative Mennonite Conference[7]	100	9,245
Impact North Ministries & Christian Anishinabec Fellowship	13	189
True Vine Christian Fellowship	5	560
Total		**9,994**
Total of all Conservative Mennonite Groups		**30,694**

Most statistics are taken from the 1996 Mennonite Yearbook.

Notes for Table

1. This group is also known as the Fellowship Churches.
2. Whereas the Ohio-Indiana Conference of Wisler Mennonites is associated with Old Order Mennonites, the Ohio Wisler Mennonites identify with conservative Mennonites.
3. These churches associate with some or all of the organized groups in this section but are not officially a part of any of them.
4. This is a very loose fellowship without formal membership.
5. The figures include churches which relate to the Bible Mennonite Fellowship but are not actually members of the group. Three Churches with a total of 165 members are full members of the group.
6. Membership in this group is informal and subject to various levels of commitment. All but two of the churches relating to the Keystone Mennonite Fellowship are members of the Lancaster Conference of the Mennonite Church.
7. Since the groups in this category do not make outward non-conformity to the world mandatory they are quite different from the other groups on the chart and have hence not been enumerated separately. Many individuals and a few churches in this category do observe a degree of traditional Mennonite outward separation.

use of radios, many do tolerate them. Moderate conservatives use Sunday school material from Christian Light Publications.

The intermediate-conservatives are not quite as strict as the ultra-conservatives, but are generally more inclined to agree with ultra-conservative thought and practice than the moderate-conservatives.

The fundamental-conservatives adhere to basic conservative Mennonite beliefs and practices, but patterns of dress are more subject to individual interpretation. Typically, women do not cut their hair or wear slacks, but capes on dresses are not required.

Theological-conservatives emphasize doctrinal orthodoxy but do not necessarily insist on traditional Mennonite practices such as plain dress and a cappella singing. The largest group in this class is the Conservative Mennonite Conference which is described in chapter six.

The Conservative Mennonite Movement cannot be understood without an acquaintance with the individual groups of which it is

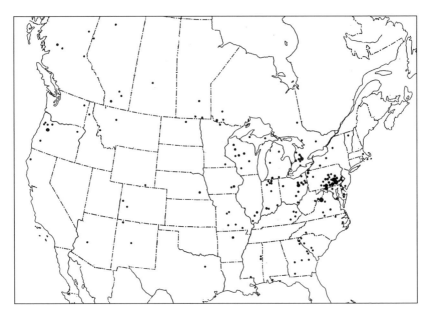

Conservative Mennonite Movement Churches, 1996.

composed. This chapter introduces each of the groups according to the circle of fellowship with which they identify. Chapter nine focuses on the distinctive beliefs and practices of congregations and groups in the Conservative Mennonite Movement.

Ultra-Conservative Groups

The Conservative Mennonite Fellowship

The conservative movement of the second half of the 20th century ironically involved many churches which had never fully joined the Mennonite Church. As noted in chapter six, the Conservative Amish Mennonite Conference and the Ontario Amish Mennonite Conference consisted of churches with Amish background, who had refrained from joining the progressive Amish Mennonites. Most of the churches in these two independent conferences ultimately moved closer and closer to the Mennonite mainstream in practice and organization. However, a conservative minority of members resisted the move.

In 1956, Bishop Valentine Nafziger led a conservative faction out of the Riverdale congregation of the Ontario Amish Mennonite

Conference to form the Bethel Conservative Mennonite Church of Millbank, Ontario. This marked the beginning of the Conservative Mennonite Movement. Also in 1956 Andrew Stutzman and all of the members of the Zion Conservative Mennonite Church of Benton, Ohio, withdrew from the Conservative Mennonite Conference. The same year the majority of the members of the Maple Grove Conservative Conference Mennonite church in Starke County, Ohio, formed the Hartville Conservative Mennonite Church. These three churches, all of whom had Amish background and had never become part of the larger Mennonite Church, organized the Conservative Mennonite Fellowship (CMF), which held its first annual meeting on June 22 and 23, 1957. [1]

Soon other churches of Amish background, mostly from the Conservative Conference, joined the CMF. Throughout the 1960s, various congregations of Mennonite Church background (sometimes called "Old" Mennonites) in Wisconsin, Ohio, and Pennsylvania also affiliated with the Conservative Mennonite Fellowship. The CMF

The Bethel Conservative Mennonite Church of Millbank, Ontario, may be considered the very first church in the Conservative Mennonite Movement. This congregation was organized in January 1956 by a group that decided to withdraw from the Ontario Amish Mennonite Conference (later Western Ontario Mennonite Conference).

established a number of home mission churches. By 1966 there were 22 congregations with 905 members.[2]

Even before the first meeting of CMF, members of the new group had seen the need for a monthly publication which would "cry out against the apostasy of our times and hold up the New Testament standard of holiness."[3] Thus the *Herald of Truth* (not to be confused with John F. Funk's earlier publication) began publication in April, 1957, at Hartville, Ohio. The name was changed to *Fellowship Messenger* in 1963 and continued publication until 1970.

Perhaps the most well known endeavor of the Conservative Mennonite Fellowship has been the Messiah Bible School. This winter Bible school began in 1958 and was held at various locations until the 1962-1963 term when it located permanently at Carbon Hill, Ohio.[4] Messiah was the first of several winter Bible schools in the Conservative Mennonite Movement and drew students from a wide variety of churches all over North America and beyond.

The Conservative Mennonite Fellowship also established a mission board and sent missionaries to Chimaltenango, Guatemala, in 1964 to work in highland Indian villages. The first converts were baptized in 1968. However, on September 14, 1981, a tragedy occurred at the Conservative Mennonite Mission in Palama, Guatemala. Missionaries John and Marie Troyer were forced out of their home at midnight by guerillas who accused them of being rich Americans. The mission vehicle was set afire, and the house was looted. Despite hours of trying to convince the guerillas that their motives were pure, John Troyer and fellow missionary Gary Miller were shot while Marie and five small children watched. Troyer died.[5]

Other missionaries eventually returned to Palama, but the local villagers urged them to leave for their own safety when guerilla activity resumed. After severe threats and the imprisonment of one person, the conservative Mennonites left Palama and relocated at Tecpan where a Mennonite church was continued.[6]

After a decade of growth and expansion, the Conservative Mennonite Fellowship began a period of decline in the 1970s that has continued to the present. Several of the churches experienced divisions, and many others withdrew from CMF or were disfellowshiped. Former CMF churches have become part of the Nationwide Fellowship, the Mid-West Fellowship, and the Bethel Conservative Fellowship. Others have chosen to remain independent. None of the three churches that began CMF are currently affiliated with the group. By 1995 CMF had only 279 members in 7 churches.[7] Since the early 1990s the Nationwide Fellowship and the Ohio Wisler Mennonite Churches (see page 177) have helped CMF with the administration of Messiah Bible School.

The Nationwide Mennonite Fellowship (Fellowship Churches)

Independently, and almost simultaneously, conservative minorities in widely scattered regional conferences of the Mennonite Church came to the point where they had had enough of what they considered compromise and apostasy. They were disenchanted with the conference structure and its failure to deal with drift. They decided to launch out on their own.

In 1959 small conservative groups withdrew from the Virgina Conference and the Ontario Conference. The following year similar conservative factions departed from the Lancaster and Pacific Coast Conferences. Other congregations scattered across the continent also joined the exodus.

A group of eighteen ordained men from conservative enclaves in Ontario, Pennsylvania, and Virginia met at Bright, Ontario, on December 15 and 16, 1959, to discuss how they might support each other. A number of topics were addressed to determine if there was unity of conviction—church offices, women's roles in the church, visiting speakers in churches, educational programs, literature programs, missions, the unequal yoke, insurance, television and radio, musical instruments, special singing, slides and motion pictures, tobacco, entertainment, sports, weddings, and funerals.[8]

A much larger subsequent meeting of Mennonites concerned about "the drift and falling away from the faith, both in doctrine and practice, so evident throughout our beloved Church" was held at Nappanee, Indiana, on March 1 to 3, 1960. Over 200 people attended, including 65 ordained men.[9] At a third meeting of the group at North Lima, Ohio, on August 12 to 14, 1960, an official statement was drafted, "We hereby register our intention to stand fast, by God's grace, on His eternal Word, following the early church in their example of (1)evangelism, (2)instruction, and (3)discipline, walking in God's standard of holiness, regardless of the culture in which we live (Titus 2:11-14)."[10]

These meetings marked the beginning of what would be variously known as the Nationwide Fellowship, Continent-Wide Fellowship,

Fellowship meetings were instituted in the Conservative Mennonite Movement to provide encouragement and direction for the widespread groups. The scene above shows the 1986 Nationwide Fellowship Meeting at Wellesley, Ontario.

or simply Fellowship Churches. Today, the most commonly used title is Nationwide Fellowship (NWF). This group was very similar to the Conservative Mennonite Fellowship. In fact, many of the early leaders of the Nationwide Fellowship participated in CMF meetings both before and after they withdrew from the Mennonite Church.

Because the Nationwide Fellowship Churches were so widely scattered, five regional fellowships were organized in the Southeast, Midwest, Northwest (western Canada), Northeast (the Mennonite Christian Brotherhood), and Ontario (the Conservative Mennonite Church of Ontario). Today, there are only four regional fellowships because the Ontario group is no longer part of the Nationwide Fellowship.

Nationwide Fellowship Meetings for the whole brotherhood were held annually until 1989. The regional groups now each have their own fellowship meetings and large international meetings are no longer held. Although church government is strongly congregational, the ordained members of all the Fellowship Churches continue to hold an international yearly meeting to establish matters of policy.

Over the years the NWF Churches have gained individual members and entire congregations from other conservative Mennonite

groups. Several churches once affiliated with the Conservative Mennonite Fellowship joined the NWF. NWF churches have also been established among the conservative Russian Mennonites in the Canadian provinces of Manitoba, Saskatchewan, and Alberta.

NWF churches have been very committed to foreign missions. There are currently (1994) six mission churches in the Dominican Republic, two in Mexico, six in Nigeria, and four in the Phillipines. Each of the four regional fellowships sponsors missions in one of the countries named and publishes a newsletter to keep the membership informed about the activities of the missions. From its very beginning, NWF has also emphasized moving to new areas and planting churches. Soon after the movement began, NWF members settled in British Columbia in 1962. Other new settlements were started in Paraguay in 1970, New Mexico in 1973, Wyoming in 1991, and California in 1994.

Nationwide Fellowship Churches have been very active in the publishing field. Three independent publishers are sanctioned by the group: Rod and Staff Publishers at Crockett, Kentucky; Lamp and Light Publishers at Farmington, New Mexico; and Grace Press at Ephrata, Pennsylvania.

Conservative Mennonite Church of Ontario

The Conservative Mennonite Church of Ontario (CMCO) was organized in 1960 by people who had withdrawn from the Ontario

The Bethel Mennonite Church of Kidron, Ohio, was formed in 1952 by a group of conservative members who withdrew from the Sonnenberg (Swiss) Mennonite Church when this church, which had always been unaffiliated, decided to join the Virginia Conference of the Mennonite Church. The Bethel Church at first associated somewhat with nearby Wisler Mennonites but later affiliated with the Nationwide Mennonite Fellowship.

Conference of the Mennonite Church. The CMCO became one of the regional divisions of the Nationwide Mennonite Fellowship. However, in the early 1990s the CMCO was disassociated from the NWF after a long disagreement over church standards. Several congregations have retained their affiliation with the NWF, and one of the oldest churches chose to be unaffiliated. Despite these losses, the CMCO counted 347 members in nine churches in 1995.[11] The Pineview Church in the Rainy River region of northern Ontario was begun by Wisler and Markham-Waterloo Conference Mennonites in 1963. This church affiliated with the CMCO in 1980 and started the Woodside Church as a branch congregation in 1987. Some people from the former Reinlander Mennonite community (a group of Russian Mennonite background) have also joined conservative Mennonite churches in this part of Ontario in recent years. Many members of the CMCO in Waterloo County have a background in the Markham-Waterloo Conference (an Old Order group described in chapter three).

Since its disassociation from the Nationwide Fellowship group, the CMCO has explored affiliation with other conservative Mennonites and has had especially close relationships with the Eastern Pennsylvania Mennonite Church. CMCO congregations have also worked closely with the two Conservative Mennonite Fellowship churches in Ontario.

The Conservative Mennonite Gospel Mission was begun by the CMCO in 1965 as an outreach to Ojibwa people in northern Ontario. The mission also started a Russian literature ministry in the 1990s. A separate mission organization sponsored by the CMCO administers the India Conservative Mennonite Church which has ministered in India since 1981.

The *Ontario Informer*, a small monthly newsletter, has been published by the CMCO since 1973. Twelve Christian schools are operated by the group with a total enrollment of 341 in 1992.

Washington-Franklin Mennonite Conference

The Washington County, Maryland and Franklin County, Pennsylvania Mennonite Conference (to use the full name) bears several notable distinctives: 1) the conference does not consider itself a break from another group but a continuation of the Washington-Franklin Conference of the Mennonite Church founded in 1790; 2) it is the most conservative group in the Conservative Mennonite Movement; and 3) it contains some of the largest conservative congregations though it is not the largest group.

The firmly conservative Mennonites of Washington County, Maryland, found a capable leader in Moses K. Horst (1882-1966), who became bishop in 1938. Horst was convinced that the outward symbols of non-conformity to the world as practiced by the Mennonite Church were true to scriptural principles and must be kept at all cost. Through solid biblical scholarship, articulate preaching, and firm leadership, Moses Horst led the churches in his district away from the modern trends affecting other areas of the Mennonite Church.

Tensions grew in the Washington-Franklin Conference as a widening disparity developed between the northern (Franklin County, Pennsylvania) district and the southern (Washington County, Maryland) district. The breaking point came in 1963 when Moses Horst disciplined members for helping at two independent

Mennonite missions which had been established on the eastern fringe of his district. Horst felt these missions were unauthorized and might have the potential of exerting a more liberal influence on his churches. A committee made up of representatives from other Mennonite conferences was called in to arbitrate the controversy, but Horst viewed this as unsanctioned interference according to the church discipline. Finally, as senior bishop and moderator of the Conference, Bishop Horst declared all the ministry in the northern district out of order and separated from them in 1965.

Moses Horst's Washington-Franklin Conference consisted of 597 members in nine congregations, all in Maryland, at the time of the separation. For several years, there was a Washington-Franklin (North) and a Washington-Franklin (South) conference, but then in 1979 the North Conference changed its name to the Franklin Mennonite Conference, which relates to the Mennonite Church General Assembly. It is noteworthy that the majority of churches descending from the original Washington-Franklin Conference, which now includes congregations affliated with a half dozen different groups, have identified with the Conservative Mennonite Movement. This phenomenon occurred in no other regional conference of the Mennonite Church.

The Washington-Franklin Conference again became true to its name in 1982 when the Waynecastle congregation was established in Franklin County, Pennsylvania. This church and seven of the eight churches that form a circle around Hagerstown, Maryland, have continued to follow an early Mennonite practice of having church services only every other Sunday morning at each meetinghouse. All members, however, attend services somewhere every Sunday morning. Sunday evening services are held at three or four meetinghouses where services had not been held in the morning.

Some members of the Washington-Franklin Conference independently began a program for giving aid to refugee families. This project had the support of the ministry but was not an official conference function. A man from Haiti joined the group through the refugee program and went back to his native land where a mission church was established in 1993. The Washington-Franklin Conference also started a mission outreach at Manchester, Kentucky, in 1978. Some members of the conference had organized the distribution of clothing to this poverty-stricken area of Appalachia. In order to receive clothing, folks were required to attend a church service conducted by the group. Soon a group of local people asked that regular services be held in their community.

Education of children of the church has been a top priority of the Washington-Franklin Conference. Paradise Mennonite School was established in 1958. Hillside Mennonite School was started in Washington County in 1989 to relieve overcrowding at Paradise. The two schools had a total enrollment of 434 in grades 1 to 11 in 1993. Two smaller schools are also maintained by the group at Flintstone, Maryland, and Manchester, Kentucky.

Other programs of the Washington-Franklin Conference are a prison ministry program, the Mennonite Old People's Home at Maugansville, Maryland (founded 1923), Mutual Fire Aid, and the Auto Aid Plan. The *Brotherhood Builder* was started as the official conference publication in 1992.

Eastern Pennsylvania Mennonite Church

The Lancaster Conference of the Mennonite Church had always been a bulwark of conservatism, but the great waves of change that began among Mennonites in the midwest finally reached Lancaster by the 1950s. While the written discipline of the conference showed little sign of erosion, there was widespread lack of enforcement of the rules. Those few bishops who insisted on consistently abiding by the conference discipline encountered increasing opposition.

In 1959 the Lancaster Confernce Bishop Board prevented Bishop Benjamin Eshbach of the Manor District from expelling 26 members of a single congregation for owning televisions.[12] Another problem arose in 1966 when Bishop Eshbach informed the Bishop Board that he could not conscientiously serve communion to members who did not comply with the conference dress standards.[13] The board instructed Eshbach to proceed with communion, but he was given the privilige to announce that he did not approve of any disobedience among the members. Bishop Eshbach felt he could not be true to his convictions if he carried out this directive. Four other Lancaster Conference bishops supported Eshbach in his stand— Homer Bomberger, Simon Bucher, Isaac Sensenig, and Aaron Shank.[14]

These five bishops decided to organize a separate Voluntary Service program for conscientious objectors which would maintain more conservative standards than the VS units maintained by the Lancaster Conference. Born in the fall of 1966, this new conservative organization was called the Mennonite Messianic Mission. This gave rise to the name "Three-M Mennonites" for the emerging group.

The five conservative bishops and their supporters continued to work with the Lancaster Conference for a time. Then in 1968 a new church discipline was adopted by the Lancaster Conference which no longer made television ownership a test of membership. The new discipline was also not as imperative about distinctive plain dress. Almost immediately the five bishops heading the Mennonite Messianic Mission resigned from the Lancaster Conference. Late in 1968 Bishops Bomberger, Bucher, Eshbach, Sensenig, and Shank agreed on the name Eastern Pennsylvania Mennonite Church for their new group. They drew up a discipline.

At the spring 1969 session of the Lancaster Mennonite Conference, the withdrawal of 47 ordained men who identified with the Eastern Pennsylvania Church was recognized.[15] By late 1969, 27 congregations were organized under the Eastern Pennsylvania Mennonite Church with a total of 1,181 members.[16] In 1995 there were 59 churches with 3,434 members. Thirty-one of the churches were in Pennsylvania, sixteen in ten other states, and twelve in four other countries.[17] The EPMC is by far the largest conservative Mennonite group.

The Blue Rock Mennonite Meetinghouse near Millersville, Pennsylvania, was built in 1970, but the congregation began in 1966 as the Sheep Lane Mennonite Church, which was a conservative congregation within the Lancaster Mennonite Conference. Blue Rock was one of the charter members of the Eastern Pennsylvania Mennonite Church.

The Mennonite Messianic Mission of the EPMC became involved in foreign mission work through other older conservative Mennonite groups. Because of lack of staff and funds, the Conservative Mennonite Fellowship was unable to expand its mission work in Guatemala. In 1970 they asked the Eastern Pennsylvania Mennonites to open new missions.[18] The EPMC established four churches in western Guatemala beginning in 1972.[19]

The four EPMC churches in British Columbia had their beginnings when the Northwest Fellowship Churches (Nationwide Fellowship) asked the EPMC to assume responsibility of a mission in 1971. This mission was originally intended for native Americans, but its resulting four congregations ultimately gained more members from the arrival of conservative Mennonites from other communities and the transfer of members from Russian Mennonite groups.[20]

The two Eastern churches in Paraguay derive from a group of people who had belonged to the Nationwide Mennonite Fellowship but affiliated with the EPMC in 1981.[21] In 1983 a mission church was established in the Bahamas on the island of Andros. This was the first Mennonite mission of any kind to be established in this country. The first convert was baptized in 1985. The EPMC missionaries have established several businesses to provide employment for poverty stricken islanders.[22]

An enthusiastic home mission ministry is carried on by the Literature-Evangelism Committee. Groups of people regularly go to urban areas like New York City and Boston to hold street meetings in which gospel literature is distributed in coordination with preaching and singing programs.[23] A church was started in the Boston area through these efforts.

The Eastern Pennsylvania Mennonite Publication Board works very closely with Rod and Staff Publishers in the preparation of tracts and school textbooks. The board is also responsible for materials produced by Eastern Mennonite Publications, including Bible school materials, Bible study helps, church history books, and parochial school materials.[24] The *Eastern Mennonite Testimony*, a monthly magazine, began publication in 1969.

Eastern Pennsylvania Mennonites operated 54 parochial schools in 1995 with a total of 184 teachers and 1,991 students.[25] Grades one to ten are offered in most schools. College attendance is strongly discouraged because of the prevailing emphasis on secularism and humanism.[26]

Numidia Mennonite Bible School was begun in 1966 by those supporting the Mennonite Messianic Mission. It became an important center for the Eastern Pennsylvania Mennonite Church.

Numidia Mennonite Bible School was started in 1966 by those involved in the Mennonite Messianic Mission. The facilities of this winter Bible School for the youth of the church have also served for many other church functions. Other programs and institutions of the EPMC are the West Willow Rest Home/Eastern Pennsylvania Mennonite Care Center (1975), the foster care program of the Child Care Committee (1980), and the Relief Committee, which gives aid to disaster victims and provides clothing and material goods for missions.

Conservative Mennonite Churches of York and Adams Counties, Pennsylvania

The York-Adams District of the Lancaster Mennonite Conference consisted of twelve congregations in the 1950s. Some of the members of the district affiliated with the Fellowship Churches in 1960 and one whole congregation became part of the Eastern Pennsylvania Mennonite Church in 1969. During the early 1970s, considerable tension arose in the district when some churches wished to follow the modern trends of the rest of the conference and others insisted on keeping the old discipline. Finally in 1975, seven of the churches in the district withdrew from the Lancaster Conference and formed a separate group called the Conservative Mennonite Churches of York and Adams Counties, Pennsylvania.

The York-Adams Conservative Mennonites have a close relationship with the Eastern Pennsylvania Mennonite Church and the Washington-Franklin Mennonite Conference. The *Statement of Christian Doctrine and Rules and Discipline of the Conservative Mennonite Churches of York and Adams County Pennsylvania* is practically identical to the written discipline of the Eastern Pennsylvania Mennonite Church. This small group has avoided merging with a larger body primarily to keep lines of fellowship open with many other parts of the Conservative Mennonite Movement. The group follows the conference form of church government, holding a conference each March and September for the ministerial body.

The Conservative Mennonites of York and Adams Counties operate two Christian Day schools. A semimonthly publication called *The Inspirational Informer* was started in 1991. The group supports a variety of mission programs, publishers, and Bible schools administered by other Conservative Mennonites.

Ohio Wisler Mennonite Churches

The Old Order Mennonites who have permitted the use of cars have much in common with the churches in the Conservative Mennonite Movement. But they also have a major difference related to manner of worship. The car-driving Old Orders have not accepted Sunday schools, revival meetings, and other evangelical practices typical of the Conservative Mennonite Movement. However, many children of recent generations of Old Order Mennonites are attracted to the newer forms of worship which their ancestors rejected in the late 1800s. These people find the Conservative Mennonite Movement inviting because of its emphases on both non-conformity to the world and evangelicalism. Many individuals from car-driving Old Order congregations have joined Conservative Mennonite Movement churches. A number of organized groups have also left Old Order conferences to form new conservative congregations.

In 1973, the four churches belonging to the Ohio-Indiana

Conference of Wisler (Old Order) Mennonites in Ohio divided. The County Line Church in Wayne County, the Maple Hill Church in Medina County, and the Salem Mennonite Church (a break from the Pleasantview Church in Mahoning County) chose to identify with the Conservative Mennonite Movement rather than the Old Order Wisler Mennonites. The new group became known as the Ohio Wisler Mennonite Churches. Two bishops from the Eastern Pennsylvania Mennonite Church have served in an advisory capacity for the Ohio Wisler Mennonites, but the churches in the group are not members of the EPMC.

Ohio Wisler Mennonites also established the new Woodlawn Mennonite Church in Richland County, Ohio. In 1995 Ohio Wisler Mennonites reported 131 households among the four churches.[27]

Intermediate-Conservative Groups

Western Conservative Mennonite Fellowship

About 1973 three churches in Oregon that had formerly belonged to the Nationwide Mennonite Fellowship (Harrisburg, Porter, and Tangent) formed a very loosely organized new group which became known as the Western Conservative Mennonite Fellowship. The Harrisburg, Oregon, church, the oldest and largest congregation in the group, began in 1911 as a conservative offshoot from the Zion Amish Mennonite Church. While Zion eventually lost its Amish identity and became part of the Pacific Coast Mennonite Conference, Harrisburg has continued to use the name Amish even though they now adhere to few distinctively Amish practices.

A congregation of former Hutterites in Alberta that had joined the Nationwide Fellowship became part of the new Western Conservative Mennonite Fellowship. Other congregations were started in Idaho, Washington, Montana, and Colorado. In 1983 the group started the Hummingbird Gospel Mission in the Central American country of Belize. Most of the churches operate their own Christian Day schools.

Bethel Conservative Fellowship

Four churches that withdrew from the Conservative Mennonite Fellowship in 1983 began a loose association that eventually adopted the name Bethel Conservative Fellowship (BCF). Three other churches later joined the Bethel Fellowship, but one of the original churches, Darbun in Mississippi, transferred to the Pilgrim Mennonite Conference in 1994 because it was geographically closer to congregations of this group.

Three BCF churches are located in Missouri, including the two largest churches. Two other churches are located in Indiana; one in Maryland; and one in Michigan. The Pelkie, Michigan, church was started by people who relocated from the Canadian province of Alberta in 1988.

The Bethel Conservative Fellowship avoids a rigid central structure but does maintain the Bethel Bible School at Seymour, Missouri, as well as a mission work in the northern part of the country of Belize called Mennonite Mission to the Americas. The Bethel Conservative Fellowship churches use Rod and Staff Sunday school materials and associate with other conservative Mennonites who do not permit radio use, especially the Western Conservative Fellowship. The Salem Mennonite Church of Keota, Iowa, relates somewhat with the BCF but does not have full membership. This church sponsors the Caribbean Light and Truth mission in southern Belize.

Pilgrim Mennonite Conference

On December 31, 1991, 22 ordained men, including bishops H. Stephen Ebersole, Sidney B. Gingerich, and Aaron M. Shank, were released from their relationship with the Eastern Pennsylvania Mennonite Church.[28] They believed the EPMC had become too legalistic in its church discipline requirements, and they wished for more activities for the young people. Several months before the official dismissal, they had organized the Pilgrim Mennonite Conference with approximately 500 members.

The Pilgrim Mennonite Conference and the Eastern Pennsylvania Mennonite Church are in basic agreement on most areas of doctrine and practice, however there are subtle differences in emphases, mainly involving church administration and discipline.

The PMC maintains a prison ministry and the "Shepherds Fold" program for released prisoners. The Evangelistic Services Committee arranges old-fashioned tent meeting revivals. The official monthly publication of the group is *The Pilgrim Witness*. There is a Relief Committee which is in charge of disaster service.

There are eight schools operated by the Pilgrim Mennonite

Conference which include grades one to ten. The Pilgrim Mennonite Bible School was established at Newville, Pennsylvania, to provide a three-week study course for youth.

The three largest congregations of the Pilgrim Mennonite Conference are located in Lebanon and neighboring Berks County, Pennyslvania. Five other churches are scattered throughout Pennsylvania, as well as one in Florida and one in Georgia. The Mt. Joy Church of Leetonia, Ohio, made up of former members of a Nationwide Fellowship church, identified with the Pilgrim Conference early in its history. The Darbun Conservative Mennonite Church transferred to the Pilgrim Conference from the Bethel Conservative Fellowship in 1994 for administrative purposes since it was close to other Pilgrim churches in the deep South.

Moderate-Conservative Groups

Cumberland Valley Mennonite Church

After the division of the Washington-Franklin Conference in 1965 (see Washington-Franklin Conference, page 171) the Franklin County, Pennsylvania, churches were known as the Washington-Franklin (North) Conference for a time. Bishop Amos E. Martin (1901-1983) became the moderator of this conference in 1965. Although Amos Martin was not as conservative as Bishop Moses Horst in the Washington-Franklin Conference of Maryland, he was still quite concerned that his members retain a non-conformed life style and appearance.

Amos Martin insisted that women wear cape dresses and comb their uncut hair up beneath a head covering of consistent size. He also asked the men to wear the regulation plain garb and forbad radios for the ministry and television in the homes of the members. A large part of the conference constituency could not accept these standards. Therefore, Martin left the Washington-Franklin (North) Conference with over 300 members and organized the Cumberland Valley Mennonite Church in 1971.

There were originally seven congregations in the Cumberland Valley Mennonite Church. The four churches in Pennsylvania were located in the northern part of Franklin County (one mission station has since closed). The members of the three Maryland churches separated from Bishop Moses Horst's southern district in 1964, before he broke away from the larger regional conference in 1965.

The Cumberland Valley Mennonite Church has been closely associated with the Southeastern Mennonite Conference. Cumberland Valley church news appears in the Southeastern periodical *Life Lines*. The Cumberland Valley churches in Maryland cooperate closely with the Hope Mennonite Fellowship. Two Christian day schools which include high school grades—one in Pennsylvania and one in Maryland—are operated by the Cumberland Valley Mennonite Church. The group strongly supports the Mennonite Air Mission in Guatemala.

Mid-Atlantic Mennonite Fellowship

Some of those who formed the Eastern Pennsylvania Mennonite Church in 1968 wished to maintain a consistent application of the 1954 Lancaster Conference discipline. Others in the group desired to improve upon the old discipline and take a more conservative route. Bishop Homer Bomberger, the second oldest of the founding bishops of the EPMC, was among those who wanted to maintain the 1954 discipline rather than becoming more conservative. The other bishops considered Bomberger too lax in discipline and assigned

Those people withdrawing from the Eastern Pennsylvania Mennonite Church in 1972 under the leadership of Bishop Homer Bomberger organized the New Haven Mennonite Church near Lititz, Pennsylvania.

two bishops to assist him with his administrative duties in October 1971. In December of 1971 Bomberger asked to be given retirement status as an EPMC bishop.[29]

A number of members in Bishop Bomberger's White Oak district supported Bomberger and felt he had been unfairly treated. These dissidents withdrew from the EPMC and started the New Haven Church near Lititz in 1972. The following year the EPMC decided that those who owned radios could no longer be members of EPMC churches. Many folks did not agree with this decision. They withdrew from the EPMC and organized the Fair Haven Church near Myerstown which came under the leadership of Homer Bomberger. In 1974 New Haven and Fair Haven had a combined total membership of 121.[30]

Bomberger's approach to Mennonite conservatism also attracted some people who were still members of Lancaster Mennonite Conference congregations. In 1977 the Sharon Mennonite Church in Lebanon County, Pennsylvania, was founded by Lancaster Conference members who wished to be under Bishop Bomberger's oversight. In 1978 the three churches under Homer Bomberger's oversight organized as the Mid-Atlantic Mennonite Fellowship. The Millmont Church in Union County and the Bairs Hostetters Church in Adams County transferred from the Lancaster Conference to the Mid-Atlantic Fellowship in 1978 and 1980 respectively.

A considerable number of Mennonites from the Weaverland (Horning) Conference, who desired a more evangelical church program but found the Lancaster Conference too liberal and the Eastern Pennsylvania Mennonites too strict, joined the Mid-Atlantic Fellowship. Most members of the Pleasant Valley Church (the largest in the group), founded in 1981, and the Blue Ball Church, founded in 1986, were of Horning Mennonite background.

The Mid-Atlantic Fellowship began an inter-city mission in Philadelphia in 1992. Support is also given to several inter-group conservative Mennonite mission endeavors.

Southeastern Mennonite Conference

The separation of the conservatives from the liberals occurred in two stages in the Virginia Mennonite Conference. The Middle District of this conference divided in 1963 ostensibly because of increased size. It was no accident, however, that the most conserva-

The Rawley Springs Mennonite Church in Rockingham County, Virginia, became part of the Southeastern Mennonite Conference when that group withdrew from the Virginia Conference of the Mennonite Church in 1972.

tive churches became part of the West Valley District and the more liberal churches were incorporated into the Central District.

After its formation, the West Valley District increasingly distanced itself from the affairs of the Virginia Conference and drew closer to other conservative groups who had recently withdrawn from the Mennonite Church. Like the Eastern Pennsylvania Mennonite Church, West Valley began its own Voluntary Service program in 1969, several years before its actual break with the Virginia Conference. Also some conservative individuals and families from other districts in the Virginia Conference began moving their membership to West Valley congregations.

The West Valley ministry persistently but futilely tried to keep the rest of the conference from following the modern trends of the larger Mennonite Church. The last straw came when the Virginia Conference revised and modernized its *Rules and Discipline* in 1970. The West Valley District could no longer conscientiously support the policies of the conference and asked to be released from its ties. This request was reluctantly granted in 1971. The West Valley District then became the Southeastern Mennonite Conference with an initial membership of 562.[31] Twelve churches identified with the new conference. In 1995, after three churches in Georgia and South Carolina organized a separate South-Atlantic Mennonite conference, there were 770 members in fourteen churches. Two mission churches were started in Puerto Rico in 1981 and 1989.[32]

Christian Light Publications in Harrisonburg, Virginia, was primarily the inspiration of one member of the Southeastern Conference, writer and editor Sanford Shank (1934-1990). While the publishing operation is privately operated and not controlled by the conference, the majority of the management and staff are members of Southeastern congregations.

Life Lines of the Southeastern Mennonite Conference began as the official conference publication in 1973.

Mid-West Mennonite Fellowship

Several widely scattered conservative Mennonite churches of rather diverse origins joined in forming the Mid-West Mennonite Fellowship in 1977. One of the primary purposes of this loose organization was the establishment of a Bible school. This objective came to fruition in 1978 when the Maranatha Mennonite Bible School was begun at Lansing, Minnesota.

The largest concentration of Mid-West Fellowship churches is located in southern Ontario. These congregations had been a part of the regional Conservative Mennonite Church of Ontario until 1976. In addition, three of the original churches in the Conservative Mennonite Fellowship—Hartville at Hartville, Ohio; Pilgrim at Middlefield, Ohio; and Bethel at Milverton, Ontario—also joined the Mid-West Fellowship. The Bethel Conservative Mennonite Church of Nappanee, Indiana, was organized by former Old Order Amish members in 1955. This congregation joined the Conservative Mennonite Conference but left this affiliation in 1969 and was independent of affiliation until it became one of the founding congrega-

The Hartville Singers from the Hartville Conservative Mennonite Church in Ohio has given a cappella concerts since the 1950s. This church is now affiliated with the Mid-West Fellowship.

tions of the Mid-West Fellowship. Similarly, the Gospel Light Chapel in Holmes County, Ohio, was made up of members who had left the Conservative Mennonite Conference in 1968 and organized an unaffiliated congregation which became part of the MWF. Several other Mid-West churches also have a Conservative Conference background. One church, Salem at Atwood, Ontario, was organized by former Beachy Amish members. Each of the other churches in the MWF scattered from northern Minnesota to southern Arizona also has its own unique story.

The Mid-West Fellowship has basically chosen not to have mission outreaches sponsored by the entire group. Rather, each congregation decides which mission endeavors to support. Northern Youth Programs is a mission outreach to the native peoples of northern Ontario, which is administered by Mid-West Fellowship ordained men. This program, consisting of a youth camp, a Bible institute, seminars, and separate high schools for boys and girls, began in 1968 as a division from the Northern Light Gospel Mission (now Impact North and Christian Anishinabec Fellowship). Fresh Start Chapel in southern Indiana is a program for delinquent youth operated by Mid-West Fellowship members. Recently, in contrast to earlier mission efforts, the Mid-West Fellowship has decided to sponsor Deeper Life Ministries, a counseling center at Plain City, Ohio.

Hope Mennonite Fellowship

During the 1970s, an Eastern Pennsylvania Mennonite bishop, Earl Horst, felt his views and convictions on various issues were not given a fair hearing within the group. After a long period of tension, he decided to withdraw from the church on May 26, 1981. About 100 members followed Horst and organized the Schaefferstown Church in Lebanon County, Pennsylvania, and the Muddy Creek Church in neighboring northern Lancaster County. A group of sympathizers from the EPMC in Illinois organized the Sunnyside Church near Wayne City at the same time. These churches formed the Hope Mennonite Fellowship which today has a close relationship with the Maryland district of the Cumberland Valley Mennonite Church.

Hope Mennonite Fellowship gained the Garber Mennonite Church (which had belonged to the York-Adams Conservative Mennonites) in 1992 but lost the Sunnyside Church in Illinois which became unaffiliated in 1993. In 1994 Hope Mennonite Fellowship consisted of four churches, all of them in Pennsylvania.

Southern Mennonite Fellowship

Outside of Virginia there had never been many Mennonite churches in the deep South, but in recent years a growing number of congregations belonging to various Mennonite groups have cropped up across the South. Several independent conservative Mennonite churches in the southeastern United States began an informal association in 1984 called the Southern Mennonite Fellowship. The primary reason for the organization was to support Heritage Bible School and Hartwell Mennonite Center both at Hartwell, Georgia.

Three of the churches identifying with the Southern Fellowship (two in Georgia and one in South Carolina) have a dual affiliation with the South Atlantic Mennonite Conference. The Faith Mission at Cuthbert, Georgia, belongs to the Conservative Mennonite Conference, but also supports the Southern Fellowship. The largest church in the fellowship is Whispering Pines at Honea Path, South Carolina, which was started in 1970 as an independent congregation, mostly by people who came from the Providence Conservative Conference Church at Virginia Beach, Virginia. The second largest Southern Fellowship church, Magnolia at Macon, Mississippi, began in 1959 as a Conservative Conference settlement made up primarily of people from the Pleasant Grove Church at Goshen, Indiana. Magnolia withdrew from the Conservative Conference in 1971.

Fair Play Christian Fellowship at Fair Play, South Carolina, developed from the Wildernesss Boys' Camp for juvenile delinquents. The workers at the camp and others who were attracted to the area because of the camp organized a congregation in 1980.

The Pinecraft Tourist Church at Pinecraft—a Mennonite and Amish retirement and winter vacation community in Sarasota, Florida—belonged to the Lancaster Mennonite Conference until 1988. At that time, it became independent and identified with the Southern Mennonite Fellowship. Sarasota Mennonite Church, located several miles east of Pinecraft, is also in sympathy with the Southern Fellowship. This church was begun in 1981 by people from various conservative Mennonite groups.

There are several other smaller churches that relate to the Southern Mennonite Fellowship, including the Gospel Light Church at Montezuma, Georgia, which was a division from the Beachy Amish Church in the area.

Unaffiliated Conservative Mennonites

Over 30 Conservative Mennonite Movement churches with a combined membership of more than 2,000 have no official ties to any of the organized groups. They are listed in the "Unaffiliated Mennonite Congregations" section of the *Mennonite Yearbook*. These churches are generally extraordinarily cautious of larger church structures and prefer to operate independently. They have various histories. Several congregations parted company with their local regional conference of the Mennonite Church and chose not to seek affiliation with a larger fellowship. Other independent conservative Mennonite churches had belonged to an organized group, but for a variety of reasons decided to sever those organizational ties. Still others resulted from schisms with churches belonging to one of the conservative Mennonite groups or other unaffiliated congregations.

Most of the unaffiliated churches do associate with conservative Mennonite groups in an informal way. The majority of these churches identify with the moderate-conservatives while a few gravitate toward the intermediate-conservatives or the fundamental-conservatives. Several are in a class all their own. Members of these churches attend meetings sponsored by the organized groups, send their young people to the various conservative Mennonite Bible schools, contribute to mission programs, and patronize conservative Mennonite publishing houses. About half of the unaffiliated churches have some association with the Mid-West Mennonite Fellowship. A smaller number relate informally to the Mid-Atlantic Mennonite Fellowship.

Space limitations prohibit telling the individual stories of each of the 30-some unaffiliated conservative Mennonite congregations. Several representative congregations are described briefly.

Holmes County, Ohio, is home to a number of unaffiliated conservative Mennonite churches, including the Faith Haven Fellowship (a 1977 division from Zion Conservative Mennonite), Gospel Haven Fellowship (a 1980 division from an Amish Mennonite group), Bethany Conservative Mennonite (a former member of the Conservative Mennonite Fellowship), and Sharon Conservative Mennonite Church (left the Conservative Conference in 1980). These four churches relate informally to the Mid-West Fellowship but are not members of that fellowship.

Holmes County's Zion Conservative Mennonite Church had been one of the charter members of the Conservative Mennonite Fellowship but withdrew from this group in 1983 and has remained unaffiliated. The congregation does have inclinations toward the Bethel Conservative Fellowship.

While several regional conferences of the Mennonite Church— Lancaster and Virginia—have witnessed large withdrawals to the conservative camps, the Ohio Conference has not experienced that same phenomenon. In fact, the Sharon Mennonite Church of Elida, Ohio, represents the only conservative offshoot from the Ohio Mennonite Conference. Sharon was organized in 1966 and had belonged to the Conservative Mennonite Fellowship for several years. This congregation now prefers to relate to a number of different conservative Mennonite groups, but is perhaps most closely associated with the Southeastern Conference because of kinship ties with Virginia.

The Haycock and Lansdale Mennonite churches divided from the Franconia Mennonite Conference in 1970. These churches have a close working relationship with each other and relate informally to the Mid-Atlantic Fellowship. The same is true of the Beth-El church of Mifflin County, Pennsylvania, which was organized by people who came out of the Allegheny Mennonite Conference in 1973 and to a lesser extent by people from the Conservative Mennonite Conference.

Lancaster County, Pennsylvania, has a wider variety of Mennonite groups than anywhere else in the world. One of the more recent additions to the array is a heterogeneous congregation called the New Covenant Mennonite Fellowship. Started in 1989 by a former Church of the Brethren minister, New Covenant was a member of the Lancaster Mennonite Conference for a short time. This independent congregation has the unique combination of adhering to conservative Mennonite practices (including women's head coverings, the prohibition of divorce and remarriage, and a ban on wearing jewelry) while encouraging the use of musical instruments, with a particular love for contemporary Christian music.

Fundamental-Conservative Groups

Bible Mennonite Fellowship

After World War II, the conservative-minded members in the Pacific Coast Conference of the Mennonite Church, began pressing for a stricter church discipline. They expressed despair over the lack of unity in practice among members of the conference. A more stringent constitution and discipline were approved by the conference in 1953, but little was done to implement its enforcement.[33]

In 1966 the conservative element proposed that the whole Pacific Coast Conference withdraw from the Mennonite Church. This recommendation was rejected by a two-to-one vote of conference delegates in 1967.[34] Later that same year the Sheridan, Bethel, and Hopewell congregations withdrew from the Pacific Coast Conference. In 1968 East Fairview and Brownsville also withdrew, followed by Fairview in 1969 and Winston in 1970.[35]

Late in 1967 some of these former members of the Pacific Coast Conference founded an organization called the Bible Mennonite Fellowship (BMF). A confession of faith, constitution, and discipline were drawn up by the leaders of the group and periodic meetings were instituted. Membership was offered to congregations and to individuals.[36]

However, congregations were slow to join the Bible Mennonite Fellowship. Individuals, especially ministers, supported the programs of the BMF, even though their congregations were not officially members. Currently, three churches with a total membership of 160 (1995) belong to the Bible Mennonite Fellowship—Brownsville and Sheridan in Oregon and Woodside in Montana. At least three other churches with a total membership of 454 identify with the BMF but are not officially members. These include the large Fairview Mennonite Church at Albany, Oregon. (One of its ministers has been the secretary of the BMF.) The group established missions in the Mexican states of Sonora and Zacatecas which have been handed over to the Hopewell Mennonite Church of Oregon (an unaffiliated church associated with the Bible Mennonite Fellowship).

The BMF confession of faith makes the following statement regarding the reasons for the formation of the group, ". . . the apparent change of belief and practice of the Mennonite Church in the areas of: inspiration and authority of the Scripture; the historic Mennonite position of nonconformity to the world; the separation of church and state; and the increased emphasis on and involvement in political and social reform."[37]

Ordained leaders in the BMF are encouraged to wear the regulation garb and are asked to refrain from wearing neckties. Members are not to "violate biblical standards by following the fashions of the world"[38] but, unlike many other conservative Mennonite groups, no definite items of required dress are specified.

Sharing Concerns Mennonite Fellowship

The Indiana-Michigan Conference has historically been one of the most progressive of the regional conferences of the Mennonite Church, and few of its churches have rejected the liberal leanings of the Conference. However, in 1971 the Sharing Concerns Bible Conference was started by several of the most conservative Indiana-Michigan congregations for the purpose of, as the name states, sharing mutual concerns. Eventually the concerns of these congregations became so great that they withdrew from the Indiana-Michigan Conference. The first to do so was Rich Valley at Kokomo, Indiana, in 1972. The largest church in the fellowship, Salem at New Paris,

Indiana, and its two daughter congregations, Toto and New Milford, severed their ties to the conference in 1981.

Other churches who today identify with the SCBC had never been part of the Indiana-Michigan Conference. The Faith Mennonite Church of Hillsdale, Michigan, had been part of the Conservative Mennonite Fellowship in its early years but now associates with Sharing Concerns. The Linn Amish Mennonite Church of Roanoke, Illinois, and the Cuba (Indiana) Mennonite Church, both of whom withdrew from the Conservative Mennonite Conference in 1996, also participate in the Sharing Concerns Bible Conference.

The churches relating to SCBC have retained many traditional Mennonite beliefs and practices, such as long hair and head coverings for women, a ban on wearing jewelry, a cappella congregational singing, and opposition to divorce and remarriage. Modest, simple dress is specified, but most churches do not insist on a uniform plain garb. The ministry does wear plain coats.

Keystone Mennonite Fellowship

By the 1980s, the great majority of churches in the Lancaster Mennonite Conference had fallen in line with the progressive ways of the larger Mennonite Church. However, a significant number of churches still wished to uphold traditional conservative standards. In 1985, a group of ministers from these churches started the Keystone Mennonite Fellowship in order to preserve and promote conservative theology and standards. This group does not want to withdraw from the conference, rather, they hope to continue raising a conservative voice. They might be said to be "in the Lancaster Conference but not of the conference."

The Keystone Fellowship established programs with a conservative emphasis as alternatives to those offered by the agencies of the larger Lancaster Conference. A separate mission board called Olive Branch Missions was started by Keystone Fellowship. A work was begun on the island of Grenada and an outreach is being started in Nigeria. Voluntary service projects are carried on in the inner city areas of York and Reading, Pennsylvania, and in rural Bradford County. There is also a summer youth camping program.

The *Keystone Mennonite Fellowship Newsletter* is a small bi-monthly publication issued from Reading, Pennsylvania. The Terre Hill Mennonite High School in Lancaster County is primarily supported by Keystone-related churches. Nearly half of the students at Faith Mennonite High School, also in Lancaster County, are from Keystone churches (most of the rest of the students are Beachy Amish). The Keystone Fellowship churches are some of the main supporters of the Sharon Mennonite Bible Institute of Harrisonville, Pennsylvania.

The churches identifying with the Keystone Fellowship still require sisters not to cut their hair and to wear head coverings consistently in public. The wearing of slacks by women is not permitted and neither sex is to wear jewelry, including wedding bands. Television is strongly discouraged. Many men wear the plain coat or lapel coats without neckties and many women wear cape dresses.

Keystone Fellowship churches express strong hesitations about the modern theological trends in the Mennonite Church. Issues of special concern to them are divorce and remarriage, accepting members who were baptized as infants without rebaptizing them, not disciplining those who served in the military, and the ordination of women.

Membership in the group is very informal. There are varying levels of commitment and support to the fellowship. About 26 Lancaster Conference churches identify with the Keystone Fellowship.

Theological-Conservative Groups

Christian Anishinabec Fellowship and Impact North Ministries

In 1938, Irwin Schantz, a member of the Lancaster Mennonite Conference, founded a mission work in northern Minnesota. By 1952, the outreach extended to the Ojibwa people of northern Ontario, and by 1965 the twelve mission churches had organized into the Northern Light Gospel Mission Conference. In 1987, seven of the churches, whose membership and leadership were predominately native peoples, organized separately as the Native Mennonite Conference. In 1995, the name was changed to Christian Anishinabec Fellowship. While the predominately white churches continued to operate under the Northern Light Gospel Mission, they did not continue as a conference. In 1993, Northern Light Gospel Mission Conference changed its name to Impact North Ministries.

The primary goals of Northern Light Gospel Missions were evangelization and planting churches. From the beginning, the mission held to very conservative Mennonite standards, including distinctive dress styles. Today the two associated groups—Christian Anishinabec Fellowship and Impact North Ministries—still emphasize doctrinal conservatism. However, in recent years members have not been required to observe traditional dress standards. These two groups are also closely associated with the Conservative Mennonite Conference. In 1995, the Red Lake Church of Impact North Ministries joined the Conservative Conference.

True Vine Christian Fellowship and Associated Churches

In 1991, the True Vine Christian Fellowship of McMinnville, Oregon, along with several associated churches, withdrew from the Pacific Coast Conference of the Mennonite Church. The churches in this group associate with each other but do not have a formal organization or an official name.

While this loose fellowship of churches is charismatic in worship style, True Vine withdrew from the Pacific Coast Conference for a number of different reasons. They stated such issues as women pastors, tolerance of homosexuals, and general lack of strong leadership and discipline as their primary grounds for disagreeing with the Mennonite Church. True Vine does not emphasize such traditional Mennonite practices as women's head coverings and distinctive dress. These churches associate with congregations that were involved in Mennonite Renewal Services, an organization of charismatic churches within the Mennonite Church which functioned between 1975 and 1995.

Fellowship of Concerned Mennonites

The publication of A Crisis Among Mennonites—In Education—In Publication by George R. Brunk, II in 1983 created considerable controversy in the Mennonite Church. Brunk pointedly charged Mennonite colleges and publishers with condoning and even promoting unorthodox teachings. He maintained Mennonite institutions were soft on modernism and hard against fundamentalism. Brunk had earlier strongly opposed a statement by the Mennonite Board of Missions in 1978 which he claimed was theologically unsound.

Brunk, like his father, had long been a crusader for conservatism as editor of The Sword and Trumpet, a monthly magazine begun in 1929 and devoted to mainitaining conservative thought and practice in the Mennonite Church. A similar publication, but even more polemical, *Guidelines for Today*, was started by western Pennsylvania bishop Sanford G. Shetler in 1965.

Those who shared the distresses of Brunk and Shetler held a mass meeting at the 1983 Mennonite General Assembly at Bethlehem, Pennsylvania. Some of the participants at this meeting held a second meeting at Berea, Ohio, in 1984 in which 99 church leaders drew up *The Berea Declaration*. The statement expressed concern that the Mennonite Church had departed from important biblical doctrines and was fraternizing with liberal elements in Protestantism. An appeal was made to the executive officers of the Mennonite Church to ". . . give immediate and serious consideration to the inroads of liberal theology upon the life of our people."[39] The 1984 Berea meeting fostered the formation of The Fellowship of Concerned Mennonites (FCM) on September 7, 1984.

Membership in the FCM is open to all who subscribe to the *Affirmation and Objectives* stated in the Constitution. This is not a denominational group, members retain affiliation with various Mennonite conferences, fellowships, and independent congregations. An Executive Committee and a Consulting Board, mostly ordained men, were established to govern the affairs of the organization. Annual FCM meetings are held at various locations and some local chapters also have public meetings. *The FCM Informer* is published bi-monthly. *The Sword and Trumpet* (which merged with *Guidelines for Today* in 1990 after the 1989 death of editor Sanford Shetler) also serves as a voice for the organization. The FCM publishes the Biblical Heritage Series of booklets which have included A *Trumpet Sound: A Crisis Among Mennonites on the Doctrine of Christ* by George Brunk II and *Biblical Perspectives on Women in Ministry* by Sanford Shetler.

Evangelical Anabaptist Fellowship

In 1983, a group of Mennonites concerned about liberal theological trends in the Mennonite Church organized the Association of Evangelical Mennonites (AEM). Some of the primary concerns were the separation of church and state, abortion, the right of the state to exercise capital punishment, feminism, and homosexuality. The focus was on conservative theology rather than on matters of conservative Mennonite practices (head coverings, dress, etc.)

Although some of the churches involved in AEM were unaffiliated, most remained in the Mennonite Church General Assembly.

A parallel organization began in Virginia independently and unknowingly of the AEM. Eric A. Kouns, a Baptist from West Virginia, was inspired by the teachings of the early Anabaptists. He became convinced that Anabaptism had a vital message for evangelicals. When Kouns came in contact with the Mennonite descendents of the Anabaptists, he concluded that many espoused modern religious liberalism and eschewed the evangelical faith he held dear.

Kouns eventually became a minister in the Virginia Menonite Conference and sought to draw together Mennonites who shared his concerns that Anabaptism and Evangelicalism were complementary to each other. Kouns helped to organize the Evangelical Anabaptist Fellowship in 1992 and became the executive secretary of the organization. This group was broader in scope than the AEM and enlisted members from several Mennonite and Brethren groups in addition to the Mennonite Church. The AEM eventually phased out with many former members becoming involved in the programs of the EAF.

The expressed purpose of the Evangelical Anabaptist Fellowship is "to promote the biblical and theological perspective of historical Anabaptism within the context of evangelical Christian Faith." The "essential compatibility and consistency of historical Anabaptism with much of contemporary Evangelicalism" is affirmed.[40] The doctrinal declarations of the EAF maintain a conservative theological stance. They believe many Anabaptist (i.e. Mennonite) scholars discourage identification with the broader evangelical community, opening the door in the Mennonite Church to theological liberalism.[41] The EAF seeks to address issues, provide a context for fellowship and education, and articulate biblical beliefs. These goals are pursued through the publication of the EAF *Newsletter*, various conferences, seminars, and workshops. In 1994 there were about 260 members of the EAF, over half of whom were pastors.

Groups Similar to Conservative Mennonites

Beachy Amish Mennonites and Related Groups

Various independent Amish Mennonite churches did not become part of the Conservative Amish Mennonite Conference.

TABLE EIGHT

Amish Mennonite Groups

Beachy Amish Mennonites	140	8,167
Mennonite Christian Fellowship	26	1,146
Independent (Kauffman) Amish Mennonites	11	app.900
Unaffiliated Amish Mennonites of		
Tennessee and Kentucky	6	app.300

These were churches who wished to be more Amish than the Conservative Amish Mennonite Conference, but were also more open to innovations than the Old Order Amish. Most of the latter group eventually became known as Beachy Amish Mennonites, named after Bishop Moses Beachy (Somerset County, Pennsylvania) who led his congregation out of the Old Order Amish in 1925.

Most Beachy Amish churches have become more and more like conservative Mennonites and have identified less and less with the Amish. In fact, some Beachy Amish churches refer to themselves simply as Mennonite. The Beachy Amish Mennonites are similar in many ways to conservative Mennonites, but they have retained some distinctively Amish characteristics, such as the men wearing beards and suitcoats with hooks and eyes.

One group of churches that is basically Beachy Amish in background and practice (although generally more conservative) has a separate organization called the Mennonite Christian Fellowship. This group is closely associated with the similarly named Mennonite Christian Brotherhood which is part of the Nationwide Mennonite Fellowship.

Another group of churches known as the Unaffiliated Amish-Mennonite Churches of Tennessee and Kentucky are similar to the Mennonite Christian Fellowship although even more conservative. This heterogeneous group was begun in 1966 by people of Beachy Amish, conservative Mennonite, and Wisler Mennonite background.

Then there are the churches descended from the followers of John Kauffman, the so-called "Sleeping Preacher," who delivered messages while in a trance. Today, these congregations may be categorized as Independent or Kauffman Amish Mennonites.

Charity Christian Fellowship

People with backgrounds in various Lancaster County "plain" groups gathered in New Holland, Pennsylvania, in 1982 to institute a church which would recapture the zeal of early Christianity and restore the original tenets of the Anabaptist movement. They wanted to make a fresh start without being encumbered by what they considered dead, meaningless traditions.

This group became the Charity Christian Fellowship. They chose not to call themselves Mennonites, but in most respects they resemble conservative Mennonites in doctrine and practice. The *Confession of Faith and Practice* of the group reveals strongly fundamentalist beliefs and support of the traditional Mennonite practices of feet washing, the devotional head covering, the holy kiss, nonswearing of oaths and opposition to military service. Baptism is usually administered by immersion. There is much freedom of expression in worship. The *Confession of Faith and Practice* states that, "We confess the nine gifts of the Holy Spirit found in I Cor. 12 to be valid though the New Testament dispensation."

There is no uniform standard of dress but brethren and sisters are instructed to, "wear modest apparel which covers and conceals the body." Further, the sisters are are to "wear a double layered garment as the Greek word 'catastola' describes." Many Charity women wear the usual cape dress worn by most conservative Mennonites, but a jacket type upper garment is also very common and is worn with a very long skirt. The type of head covering is not specified, but most women wear a large, opaque, white veiling. Most of the men have beards and wear simple, modest clothing.

Charity Christian Fellowship has carried on an aggressive program of evangelization. Many converts have been won from other Mennonite and Amish groups as well as from non-Anabaptist backgrounds. One church relating to the fellowship was started by former Hutterites in Montana. In 1993, there were nine churches in eight states relating to Charity with a total membership of approximately 500. There is also a mission in the African country of Ghana. Most of the children in the Charity-related churches are home schooled.

Crossroads Mission Church

The Crossroads Mission Church began in 1986 in the Holmes County, Ohio, Amish and Mennonite community. This church, under the leadership of Wayne Weaver, associated with the Charity Christian Fellowship of Lancaster County, Pennsylvania, but ceased full fellowship with this group in the early 1990s. Churches at Andover, Ohio; McClure, Pennsylvania; Cumberland, Virginia; and Lafayette, Georgia established a relationship with the Crossroads Mission Church. Churches in Honduras and Costa Rica also are part of the fellowship. There may be as many as 500 members altogether. In many respects the Crossroads Mission Church is somewhat similar to the Charity Christian Fellowship, but they are less restrictive and more in tune with the modern charismatic movement.

The Church of God in Christ (Holdeman) Mennonites

John Holdeman (1832-1900), a Mennonite Church member from Wayne County, Ohio, started a separate group in 1859 with emphasis on the "true lineage" of the church, evangelical conversion, church discipline, and the shunning of the excommunicated. Holdeman failed to attract many followers from those of his own background, but in the late 1800s, large numbers of recent Mennonite immigrants from Polish Russia in Kansas and many members of the Kleine Gemeinde Mennonites in Manitoba were converted to the movement.

The Holdeman Mennonites are very similar to groups in the Conservative Mennonite Movement in their amalgamation of an evangelical church program with outward non-conformity to the world. They have stayed separate from other conservative Mennonites because of their emphasis on the one true church doctrine and the use of shunning. Holdeman men have short beards and wear conventional lapel coats but no neckties. Women wear their uncut hair beneath a black covering.

The Church of God in Christ had 16,188 in 240 churches in the United States and Canada in 1995. The church also had 2,448 members in thirteen other countries.[42]

9.

The Conservative Way

Conservative Mennonites tend to be very thorough people. Many of the congregations and groups meticulously and articulately address every conceivable area of doctrine and practice in their effort to follow the full counsel of God. Their aim is complete Christian consistency. Although they believe there are true Christians in other denominations, conservative Mennonites are generally convinced that no other religious group comes closer to the true biblical faith than they do.

Quotes from the tract "People Call Us Mennonites" from Rod and Staff Publishers might serve to show how conservative Mennonites perceive themselves: "More important than being called Mennonites is the fact that we are Christians who obey the entire Gospel. . . We are willing to be different because we are serious about getting to heaven . . . We are different because we love Jesus. He gave his life for us, and we want to live our lives for Him. He has a right to tell us what to do in every area . . . We are different because we believe the Bible—every word of it . . . We are also different because we believe it is wrong for those who profess to be Christians to live in sin . . . the Bible teaches that we must continue to make a conscientious and sincere effort to walk with God every day . . . Our church has compiled a list of expressions of how a Christian can realistically express Biblical Christianity in the twentieth century . . . When you look at us, we hope it will make you think of God and help you to see Jesus as the Lamb of God which taketh away the sin of the world . . . So if you are serious about getting to heaven, come and worship with us."

Doctrine

"It is highly necessary that Christians know what are the teachings of the inspired Word, and that they make these doctrines a part of

Christian Light Publications

Numidia Mennonite Bible School

Messiah Bible School

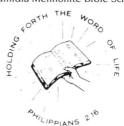

Southeastern Mennonite Conference

Pilgrim Mennonite Bible School

Sharon Mennonite Bible Institute

Eastern Mennonite Testimony

The Sword and Trumpet

Pilgrim Witness

The logos of various conservative Mennonite groups, publications, and institutions illustrate their emphasis on the centrality of the Bible.

their faith and life. It makes a difference what we believe." So states Daniel Kauffman in the introduction to *Doctrines of the Bible*[1] and so believe all conservative Mennonites. Kauffman's 1928 book is still the standard text for the study of Mennonite doctrine at conservative Mennonite Bible schools. The eighteen articles of *Christian Fundamentals* adopted at the 1921 Mennonite Church General Conference at Garden City, Missouri, serve as the confession of faith of many conservative Mennonite groups and are often printed in their official statements of doctrine. The statement was originally made in the midst of a modernist-fundamentalist controversy to establish the church on a firm biblical basis. It was not meant to replace the earlier *Dortrecht Confession of Faith* of 1632. Present-day conservative Mennonites also affirm the rediscovered *Schleitheim Confession* of 1527.

At the third annual Biblical Discipleship and Fellowship Ministerial Meeting held at Hartville, Ohio, in 1964, a restatement of the *Christian Fundamentals* was made by some of the first conservatives who withdrew from the Mennonite Church in the 1950s and early 1960s. They felt a need to address some of those areas of doctrine and Christian living which had been called into question in the years following the 1921 statement. Several conservative Mennonite groups have adopted the 1964 Hartville statement as their official confession of faith.

Conservative Mennonites agree with other conservative Christians on the basic issues of faith. The inspiration of the Bible, the Trinity, the Genesis account of the Creation, the fall of man, the virgin birth, the blood atonement, the bodily resurrection of Christ, the new birth, the indwelling of the Holy Spirit, and the assurance of salvation are all professed.

Conservative Mennonites differ from most other Christians on matters relating to separation from the world, church discipline, and what should be considered ordinances of the church. In addition to the usual ordinances of baptism, communion, and marriage, conservative Mennonites consider the literal observance of feet washing, the holy kiss, the woman's head covering, and anointing with oil as crucial to the Christian faith.

Concerning baptism, the statement of the Southeastern Mennonite Conference is representative of all conservative Mennonites, "Baptism with water shall be administered by pouring,

These views of the Blue Rock Mennonite meetinghouse near Millersville, Pennsylvania, depict the plain, simple interior typical of conservative Mennonite church buildings. Any kind of ornamentation is conspicuously absent as are musical instruments. The raised platform and pulpit are reserved for the ordained men. The lectern in front of the pulpit is for the song leader and any non-ordained speakers. Men and women sit in separate sections divided by the center aisle. The sections of folding chairs on each side of the pulpit are for Sunday school classes. Other classes are held in small rooms along each side of the main assembly room.

Sunday school is an important part of the program of Conservative Mennonite Movement churches. These quarterly lesson books from Rod and Staff Publishers demonstrate the division into various age groups for Sunday school classes.

since it symbolizes the outpouring of the Holy Spirit (Acts 2:16-18, 38; 10:44-48). Those applicants shall be baptized who have given evidence of repentance from sin, of a profession of faith, of the new birth, and of the life of discipleship in Christ. Baptism is 'the answer of a good conscience toward God' (I Peter 3:21)."[2]

Rules, Regulations, Standards, and Discipline

The final authority of the Word of God in all matters of doctrine and practice is an important tenet of conservative Mennonite faith. It is also believed that the church has the responsibilty to make specific applications of scriptural principles. The right to formulate church rules is based on the passage in Matthew 16:19 where Jesus speaks to Peter concerning administration of the church, "And I will give unto thee the keys of the kingdom of heaven: and whatsoever thou shalt bind on earth shall be bound in heaven; and whatsoever thou shalt loose on earth shall be loosed in heaven." This principle of binding and loosing is believed to give the church the authority to forbid or permit various items and behaviors for its members.

Christians in every land and age are seen to have an obligation to apply scriptural principles to daily life in the same way the early church established standards relating to the culture of that time (the example of Acts 15). It is emphasized that the Holy Spirit works through the collective body of believers in formulating these rules. It is considered safer to give priority to the discernment of the whole church body rather than the impressions and revelations of an individual. Each member is thought to need the combined counsel of the brotherhood in order to make decisions on matters of practice.

Rules and regulations are not seen as a means of salvation nor a guarantee of spirituality, but a way of giving guidance and help to Christians during their earthly sojourn. There is much caution that the rules do not contradict, add to, or replace the Bible. Conservative Mennonites are concerned that the regulation of outward practices not be the primary focus of the church. Their goal is total commitment to Jesus Christ. Their desire is to present a testimony of Christ-centered unity to the world, which they believe is achieved through uniformity of practice. The sacrifice of personal liberties is seen as a small price to pay for this unity.[3]

Compliance with the rules and regulations of the church is regarded as a test of a member's surrender to God and the church. Sinful and rebellious members are dealt with in order to maintain the purity of the church. Those who continue in disobedience to the Bible and scriptural principles, as expressed in the written discipline of the church, are to be excommunicated. A great deal of counsel and admonition normally takes place before an unrepentant member is expelled. Some sinful acts, however, may demand immediate dismissal. They include joining the military service, becoming the

Four part a cappella singing has been highly developed by conservative Mennonites.

aggressor in a divorce, or remarrying while one's partner is still living.[4]

It is hoped that through the exercise of discipline the excommunicated member will see the seriousness of his or her offense and wish to be restored to the church. Offenders may be reinstated in the church if "clear evidence of deep humility, repentance, and confession"[5] is shown.

Education

"The education of our children in a wholesome Christian atmosphere is a Biblical imperative. We believe the church should assist parents in fulfilling this responsibility by sponsoring Christian day schools with a Bible-based curriculum." So states the Eastern Pennsylvania Mennonite Church in its *Statement of Christian Doctrine.*[6]

This is the general attitude of all conservative Mennonites, and

Nearly all children from conservative homes attend Christian day schools operated by the individual churches or church groups. In some cases children are home schooled, but virtually none go to public school.

The Conservative Mennonite Teachers' Institute is an annual two-day training and inspirational meeting held at various locations across the country. The 1995 meeting shown here was at the Kralltown Mennonite School and Church near East Berlin, Pennsylvania.

virtually all churches sponsor Christian day schools, either jointly or individually. Many conservative Mennonite schools extend only through tenth grade. The Eastern Pennsylvania Mennonites explain, "We discourage our members from pursuing institutional higher education because of its emphasis on secularism and humanism."[7] Some groups and individual congregations do provide schooling through grade twelve, but very few students go on to college.

The annual Conservative Mennonite Teachers' Institute, held in various communities, and the EPMC's Teachers' Instruction Course provide training for teachers. A variety of conservative Mennonites and Amish Mennonites have recently started an institution called Faith Builders at Guys Mills, Pennsylvania, which offers a more extended teacher-training program.

The many responsibilities of the Christian school mentioned in the tract *We Believe in a God Centered School* from Rod and Staff Publishers include: 1) presenting the Bible as man's guide for moral conduct and salvation; 2) relating God's directives to each subject; 3) sensing God's demands for holy conduct; 4) disciplining ungodly conduct and practices; 5) aiming to love the soul above all other interests; 6) cautioning against the errors of secular books and

Although most conservative Mennonites are cautious of higher education, Bible schools are considered very important in indoctrinating the youth of the church. These scenes are from Messiah Bible School at Carbon Hill, Ohio, begun in 1958, as the first of several such institutions in the Conservative Mennonite Movement.

A *number of conservative Mennonite churches in the deep South cooperated in found-ing the* Heritage Bible School *of Hartwell, Georgia, in* 1986.

philosophies; and 7) employing godly teachers who are led by the Holy Spirit.

Rod and Staff maintains that public schools: 1) are operated by the government for the promotion of patriotic zeal; 2) employ non-Christian teachers who, consequently, are tools in Satan's hand; 3) teach students to strive for social acclaim and self-dependence; 4) teach that humans derive from animals; 5) ban God in most areas while promoting pagan concepts and giving the devil freedom; and 6) allow students to defy, scorn, and curse the authority of parents, teachers, and God in conversations and demonstrations. While the document which includes these points-of-view comes from Rod and Staff, an independent conservative Mennonite publishing house, various or all of these beliefs and positions are held by most conservative Mennonite groups.

Bible Schools

To provide conservative Mennonite youth the opportunity for intensive Bible study in a controlled spiritual atmosphere, a number of winter Bible schools have been established. This is a continuation of the winter Bible schools that were popular in the Mennonite Church from the early 1900s to the 1970s. The Conserative Mennonite Fellowship (CMF) started Messiah Bible School in 1958 as a more conservative alternative to the Conservative Mennonite Bible School (later Rosedale Bible Institute) operated by the Conservative Mennonite Conference. Several other conservative Mennonite groups established other Bible schools later.

Students from any affiliation may attend the Bible schools regardless of the sponsoring group. The minumum age for attendance is usually sixteen. The majority of the students are unmarried youth, but some older students attend as well. The Bible schools conduct from one to four three-week terms from December through March.

A wide range of courses are offered, including in-depth studies of individual books of the Bible as well as subjects like Nonresistance, Mennonite Church History, and Victorious Christian Living. Typically, morning and evening worship services are part of the daily schedule, and a revival meeting is held during each three-week term. Singing is an important activity at Bible schools, and most students enjoy taking part in school choruses.

TABLE NINE

Conservative Mennonite Bible Schools and Institutes

Messiah	1958	Carbon Hill, OH	Conservative Mennonite Fellowship
Numidia	1967	Numidia, PA	Eastern Pennsylvania Mennonite
Sharon	1977	Harrisonville, PA	(supported by several groups*)
Maranatha	1978	Lansing, MN	Mid-West Mennonite Fellowship
Heritage	1986	Hartwell, GA	Southern Mennonite Fellowship
Bethel	1991	Seymour, MO	Bethel Conservative Fellowship
Pilgrim	1993	Newville, PA	Pilgrim Mennonite Conference

* The Keystone Mennonite Fellowship, Mid-Atlantic Mennonite Fellowship, Southeastern Mennonite Conference, and associated independent churches are the primary administrators of the Institute.

The Sharon Mennonite Bible Institute began in 1977 and followed the pattern of Rosedale Bible Institute. However, Sharon's goal was to hold to more conservative standards than Rosedale. Sharon also offered a more advanced level of study than the other conservative Bible schools. Its terms are designed for young people of post-high school age.

Publishing

Conservative Mennonites place a high value on Christian literature. The printed word has been extensively used to instill and disseminate the conservative message. Publishing efforts have been important in the formation of conservative Mennonite groups and have been rallying points for distinct circles of fellowship among the various groups.

The Story of Christian Light Publications

One of the first organized efforts of what became the Conservative Mennonite Movement was in the area of publishing. Long before the current conservative element began withdrawing from the Mennonite Church, a loud voice of warning against creeping modernism was heard through *The Sword and Trumpet*, a periodical which George R. Brunk I began publishing in 1929 at Harrisonburg, Virginia. This publication continues to speak for conservatives who have stayed within the Mennonite Church, although the editor, George R. Brunk II, affiliated with an independent congregation in 1988.

Christian Light Publications at Harrisonburg, Virginia, was incorporated in 1969 through the efforts of Sanford Shank (center), who owned and operated Parkview Press.

Sanford Shank, a staunch conservative thinker and supporter of Brunk's publication, was the owner of a printing operation called Parkview Press in Harrisonburg, Virginia. Parkview Press regularly printed *Sword and Trumpet* and supported the concerns raised by the publication. In 1965, Shank founded Christian Light Publications as an outgrowth of *Sword and Trumpet*. The publishing operation was incorporated separately in 1969 and took over responsibility for Sunday school materials and Christian literature from *Sword and Trumpet* in 1972.[8]

Christian Light produces a full line of Christian literature, including books for adults and children and many religious tracts. Christian school curriculum materials for grades one through twelve published under the title Christian Light Education form a large part of Christian Light's offerings. A current project is to translate curriculum material into German for use among Mennonites in Mexico and the production of a Spanish curriculum in cooperation with a Costa Rican publisher. The publishing house is operated by a board of directors some of whom are members of the Southeastern Mennonite Conference, but it is not controlled by that conference. Most of what might be called the moderately conservative Mennonite churches make use of Christian Light Sunday school literature.

The Story of Rod and Staff Publishers

A number of people from the Virginia and Lancaster Mennonite Conferences started the Pilgrim Mennonite Press in 1958 as a conservative alternative to the Mennonite Church's Mennonite Publishing House. After the folks who operated Pilgrim Press withdrew from the Mennonite Church in 1959, a short-lived merger was effected with Herald of Truth Publishers at Hartville, Ohio. Paul Landis, the former chairman of Pilgrim Mennonite Press, moved to Hartville in 1959 to take charge of the operation. Later the same year, irreconcilable differences surfaced within the organization, and Landis moved to Crockett, Kentucky, where he established Rod and Staff Publishers.

Rod and Staff rapidly launched into large scale publishing, eventually including seven periodicals, Sunday school quarterlies for six age levels, school textbooks and other curriculum materials, dozens of religious tracts, doctrinal books, inspirational and storybooks,

The dissemination of sound Christian literature was a top priority from the beginning of the Conservative Mennonite Movement. Rod and Staff Publishers at Crockett, Kentucky, was founded in 1959 by Paul Landis (center).

and even Christian coloring books. *The Christian Contender,* which began in 1960 as the *Pearl of Great Price,* is the Rod and Staff general interest religious magazine. Some literature is published in German and Spanish. Rod and Staff Sunday school materials are used by a large number of conservative Mennonite churches, mostly those of the ultra-conservative vein. Rod and Staff school materials are also widely used by non-Mennonite home schools. The Nationwide Mennonite Fellowship sanctions Rod and Staff Publishers, but the publishing house is not controlled by the group.

Other Conservative Mennonite Publishing Houses

Eastern Mennonite Publications sponsored by the Eastern Pennsylvania Mennonite Church at Ephrata, Pennsylvania, works closely with Rod and Staff Publishers in producing Bible school materials, Bible study helps, church history books, and parochial school materials.[9]

Lamp and Light Publishers was founded in 1974 in Farmington, New Mexico, by members of the Conservative Mennonite Fellowship who later changed affiliation to the Nationwide Fellowship. Lamp and Light has focused on home Bible study courses and Spanish language materials.

Grace Press at Ephrata, Pennsylvania, began in 1986 as another publisher supported by the Nationwide Fellowship. The special mission of this operation has been to produce Gospel literature in the Russian language. Even before the fall of communism in the Soviet Union, thousands of Russian New Testaments printed at Grace Press were distributed behind the Iron Curtain.

Many of the conservative Mennonite groups produce their own periodicals. Some of these are rather small newsletters with a few inspirational articles while others are more extensive religious magazines. A number of mission orgaizations also publish newsletters.

Missions

Conservative Mennonites believe "That the church is commanded to evangelize the world that her primary mission is to deal with that which is spiritual and eternal." Further, "That Christian disciples are concerned also with human needs which are physical, emotional, mental, and social."[10] A variety of home and foreign missions are operated by conservative Mennonite groups and individual congregations.

TABLE TEN

Conservative Mennonite Movement Missions

Supporting Congregation or Group	Location	Founded
Bethel Conservative Fellowship		
(Mennonite Witness to the Americas)	Belize	1984
Bible Mennonite Fellowship	Mexico	1982
Conservative Mennonite Church of Ontario		
(Conservative Mennonite Gospel Mission)	Ontario Ojibwa	1965
(India Conservative Mennonite Church)	India	1981
Conservative Mennonite Fellowship	Guatemala	1964
Eastern Pennsylvania Mennonite Church		
(Mennonite Messianic Mission)	Guatemala	1970
	British Columbia	1971
	Paraguay	1981
	Bahamas	1983
Keystone Mennonite Fellowship		
(Olive Branch Missions)		
	Grenada	1988
	Nigeria	1993
Mennonite Air Missions*	Guatemala	1972
Nationwide Mennonite Fellowship	British Columbia	1962
	Paraguay	1970
(West Indies Witness)	Dominican Republic	1981
(Open Door Ministries)	Mexico	1982
(Nigeria Witness)	Nigeria	1982
(Philippine Witness)	Phillipines	1982
Northern Youth Programs*	Ontario Ojibwa	1968
Salem Mennonite Church (Keota,IA)		
(Carribean Light and Truth)	Belize	1974
Sonlight Mennonite Missions*	Haiti	1968
	Romania	1994
Southeastern Mennonite Conference	Puerto Rico	1981
Washington-Franklin Mennonite Conference	Haiti	1993
Western Conservative Mennonite Fellowship		
(Hummingbird Gospel Mission)	Belize	1983

* These independent mission organizations are supported by some or all of the following groups: Cumberalnd Valley Mennonite Church, Mid-Atlantic Mennonite Fellowship, Mid-West Mennonite Fellowship, Southeastern Mennonite Conference, Keystone Mennonite Fellowship, independent conservative Mennonite churches.

Conservative Mennonites have been very zealous in establishing home and foreign missions. A number of outreaches have been established among the Ojibwa people of northern Ontario. The young man shown above shares the Gospel message through his work in the Northern Youth Programs of Dryden, Ontario.

The distribution of Gospel tracts is a ministry many churches engage in. A tract rack is typically found in the meetinghouses of Conservative Mennonite Movement congregations.

Southeastern Conference Mennonites in Virginia join in cutting and drying apples for relief work.

The Christian and the Government

Conservative Mennonites are among the most law abiding citizens in North America. They are as scrupulous about obeying the secular government as they are about complying with their own church standards. The discipline of the Eastern Pennsylvania Mennonite Church states, "Members should at all times pray for their rulers and maintain an attitude of submission to the government under which they live, whether the demands made by the said government seem reasonable or unreasonable."[11] An even stronger statement was made in the tract *The Christian's Relation to the Nation*, "To disobey the civil authority's laws when they do not conflict with the higher authority of God is to bring upon us both the punishment of the state and the damnation of God."[12] As this statement implies, there are limits to civil obedience. When the decrees of the government conflict with holy writ, it is believed that the Christian should ". . . obey God rather than men."[13]

Conservative Mennonites believe that the church and the state are completely separate. It is acknowledged that God chose to work through the nation of Israel during Old Testament times but this entirely changed with the coming of Christ. In the words of Jesus, "My kingdom is not of this world. . . "[14] Christians are seen as aliens in a foreign land no matter where they might live. They are also called to be ambassadors for Christ's heavenly kingdom.

Conservative Mennonites take a very strong stance against participation in the military. The words of Christ are given to support their complete opposition to taking up arms, "My kingdom is not of this world: if my kingdom were of this world, then would my servants fight. . . "[15] "Put up again thy sword into his place: for all they that take the sword shall perish with the sword."[16] The Sermon on the Mount is taken literally when it says, ". . . love your enemies, bless them that curse you, do good to them that hate you, and pray for them which despitefully use you, and persecute you"[17] and "But I say unto you, That ye resist not evil: but whosoever shall smite thee on thy right cheek, turn to him the other also."[18] The belief in "non-resistance" comes from this passage, a vital Mennonite doctrine.

Conservative Mennonites practice absolute non-resistance and forbid any involvement with the military, whether combatant or non-combatant service. The ruling of the Eastern Pennsylvania Mennonite Church speaks for virtually all conservative Mennonites, ". . . members who go into military service or training forfeit their membership."[19] From the 1950s to the 1970s, while military conscription was in effect, conservative Mennonite young men took part in the I-W alternate service program in the United States. Conscientious objectors were permitted to serve two years in civilian jobs for the public welfare at this time. Some conservative Mennonite groups operated voluntary service units where young men lived while working for minimal pay on their alternate service jobs.

Although conservative Mennonites might be termed pacifists, they do not identify themselves as such. The term non-resistance is considered more Biblical and more appropriate to their stance. The theological implications of non-resistance as opposed to pacifism have been strong points of contention between the conservative and liberal elements in the Mennonite Church.

Conservative Mennonites associate modern pacifism with the idea of peace through social and political reform. They believe true peace can only be achieved by the regeneration of individuals.

Pacifists are also faulted for trying to achieve their goals by working through government officials. Foisting Christ's way of peace on unregenerate governments is deemed futile. The non-violent resistance of many pacifists is regarded as a means of force foreign to true Biblical non-resistance.

It is the general conservative Mennonite belief that government officials rule by divine authority as ministers and servants of God but not as sons of God. The government is therefore not required to abide by Christian principles, including non-resistance. On the basis of Romans 13:1-5, conservative doctrine states, "The state is to keep order in an unregenerate society by terrorizing evil, revenging evil, executing wrath upon the evildoer, and the use of capital punishment for serious offenses."[20] Therefore, secular governments are seen to have the right to maintain military and police forces to take care of their own ungodly realm. Christians, however, are viewed as citizens in God's higher kingdom, and are thus aliens to all earthly nations. This is the reason conservative Mennonites do not vote in civil elections, hold political offices, or serve on juries. Not only is voting seen as interfering in the affairs of the kingdoms of this world, but the act of voting is regarded as an indirect involvement with the government's law enforcement and military functions.

Since the church and the state are understood to be in two different spheres, conservative Mennonites feel they would be totally out of place telling the government how to handle its business. Christian involvement in lobbying, protesting, and demonstrating are considered entirely inappropriate. In turn, conservative Mennonites believe the government has no right to interfere in the affairs of the church.

Conservative Mennonites also believe that when Christ said ". . . Render therefore unto Caesar the things which are Caesar's; and unto God the things that are God's," he meant for his followers to pay any taxes that the government asked of them. As one writer explains, ". . . when the nation asks for it, we give it to them and it is never our responsibility to tell the government how it may use its money. If I owe a person some money, I have no right to refuse to pay it on the grounds that he will not use it properly. Nor can I refuse to pay it unless he promises to use it the way I say he should."[21] This statement was no doubt made in response to the trend in modern Mennonite circles to withhold tax monies used for military purpos-

The elderly are valued and respected among conservative Mennonites. Many groups secure exemption from social security, feeling that it is the church's responsibility to care for the aged.

es and, further, to instruct the government in how it should use tax monies. For conservative Mennonites, however, the line is drawn at war bonds, which are seen as voluntary investments in a war program.

As part of their belief in non-resistance, conservative Mennonites also do not believe in suing each other or those outside the church. Neither is declaring bankruptcy considered an option. Involvement with labor unions is objectionable, not only because of the "unequal yoke" with unbelievers, but also because of the frequent use of coercion and force by such organizations. To be completely consistent in non-resistance, many conservative Mennonites further have convictions against posting no trespassing signs on their farm properties because the signs usually threaten prosecution by the law.[22]

The early Anabaptists firmly believed that Christians were not to swear to any kind of oaths because the Bible says "Swear not at all."[23] Conservative Mennonites continue to have this conviction, and on those rare occasions when they are asked to swear an oath, they affirm that what they are saying is true rather than to swear. It is their contention that "An oath is not needed by an honest man, nor will an oath make a dishonest man truthful."[24] They object to having their members join secret societies and lodges because, among other things, these organizations usually require the swearing of oaths.

Young People's Activities

In an article entitled, "Protecting Our Young People," an Eastern Pennsylvania Mennonite bishop writes, "We must help them to be happy with a manner of life that reflects obedience to the Bible and deliverance from the devastations of lustful living. As parents, we should be rejoicing that our children are surrounded by influences coming from church, school, and other Christian homes that encourage true values, purity, and proper moral development."[25] The Eastern Pennsylvania Mennonite Church feels strongly that social activities among youth need to be carefully controlled. Actually, this group has no activities specifically for youth, but most of the participants in some church functions are predominately youth. Some church districts have sanctioned choruses, made up almost entirely of single youth. Special caution is taken to ensure that chorus practice sessions do not become merely social occasions. Most of the participants in the literature distribution programs are single youth as are the students at winter Bible schools. The EPMC does not

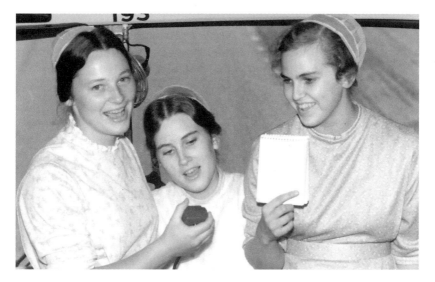

Singing is a favorite activity among conservative Mennonite youth. These Virginia young women enjoy an impromptu song on a bus trip.

allow youth to take part in organized ball games. Very casual family ball games are permissible, but youth gatherings for the express purpose of ball playing are taboo. It is felt that game playing should decrease after a young person makes a Christian commitment. By dating age, there should be little if any sports activity, except perhaps in a limited way at home.[26]

The Nationwide Fellowship churches, the Washington-Franklin Conference, and like-minded groups have views similar to the EPMC on youth activities. The groups that have withdrawn from the EPMC, along with other more moderate conservatives are less restrictive, but still cautious about youth activities. The Pilgrim Mennonite Conference states, ". . . excessive social activities will choke out spiritual growth and productivity, and play activities primarily are for children. . . " This group discourages group use of public athletic facilities, social activities that go late on Saturday evenings, and after church physical play activities.[27]

Courtship and Marriage

Sound moral standards and personal holiness are imperative to all conservative Mennonites. This is especially true in regard to courtship and marriage. Special effort has been given to providing youth with guidelines to help them see the seriousness of seeking a life's companion.

First, the choice of marriage partners is limited. The Southeastern Mennonite Conference stipulates, "Marriage should be only in the Lord. The Christian should never think of marrying an unbeliever. So important is spiritual harmony in marriage that even a denominational difference puts an unnecessary strain on the marriage relation."[28] The same group also declares another tenet of all conservative Mennonites, "Divorce and remarriage or marriage to a divorced person whose spouse is still living, being adultery, violates the symbolism of marriage and is both morally and scripturally wrong. It disqualifies one for church membership."[29]

The Eastern Pennsylvania Mennonite Church recommends that there be no dating until age eighteen. "General association with other young people in the midteen years is much more desirable and beneficial than exclusive friendships." It is advised that a young person seek the guidance of God and the counsel of parents and ministers before dating. Dating only once every two weeks is thought to be best. Initially, letters are suggested as a way to communicate between dates. Late night dates, dimly lit rooms, and isolation from others on dates are strongly discouraged. Sunday afternoon is thought to be the best time for courtship. Concerning intimacy, "Do not express your affection for each other by sitting together too close, holding hands, or engaging in similar conduct. Physical contact in courtship begins a process that is very hard to reverse. It tends to cloud your judgment and make it easy for you to mistake mere physical attraction for a properly growing friendship. It has taken many a young couple down a road that they never intended to travel." Activities considered proper and profitable for dating are church functions, singing, discussing Sunday school lessons, reading the Bible, and praying.[30]

With the lifelong commitment of marriage in mind, it is advised that a courtship continue for at least two years in order to be assured that the relationship is under the blessing of God. Because of the intensity of the engagement relationship, it is thought that the engagement time itself should be short—no longer than six months.[31]

The propriety of the wedding ceremony and reception has been a prime concern of conservative Mennonites. It seems that many young couples have trouble curbing their desires for pomp and frivolity. The written disciplines of many church groups devote considerable space to wedding guidelines. It is emphasized that the wedding be a serious time of worship. The Southeastern Mennonite Conference declares, "The popular wedding is very much a bride-centered affair; and very often a great deal of extravagance and display is expended upon it. The Christian wedding in contrast should be Christ centered."[32] The Eastern Pennsylvania Mennonites specify that the bride's dress shall be of the usual cape style and not of a special design. White wedding dresses are the norm in this and most other conservative Mennonite churches. The regular head covering, rather than a bridal veil, is worn. All those taking part in the wedding are to wear the regulation garb. The bridal group takes its place in the auditorium before the service begins, and there are no bridal marches either when entering or leaving. Only congregational singing from the regular church hymnals is permitted. The wedding service follows the pattern of a regular worship service with a devotional period and Biblical message followed by the marriage

Simplicity and sobriety are very much stressed in conservative Mennonite weddings. A bit of decoration is not considered inappropriate.

ceremony. The bishop in charge asks the marriage vow questions of the bride and bridegroom to which they respond with simple answers. In order to emphasize that the vows are made to God, the bride and groom are not to repeat the vows to each other. "We believe that the binding power of any marriage rests in the solemn and unfeigned vows given between man and woman in Christian faith. Therefore, the ring ceremony "has no part in the Christian wedding" so states the Southeastern Mennonite Conference.[33] The standards of the Mennonite Christian Brotherhood declare, "Personal intimacies, such as embracing and kissing between husband and wife, are not for public display." There is a reception line for guests to meet the newlyweds. No picture taking is allowed in the auditorium at any time. The Mennonite Christian Brotherhood admonishes, "Rice and confetti throwing, decorated cars, hilarious conduct, and horn blowing destroy our witness in our communities and bring reproach to God's people."

At the reception, the EPMC recommends the singing of congregational hymns before and after the meal. Special singing and recorded music are not allowed. Flowers and greens on tables are kept at a minumum, and there are to be no candles or cakes on display.

224

Conservative Mennonite newlyweds go on wedding trips (the term "honeymoon" is considered un-Christian). The EPMC recommends that places having educational value or natural beauty be included on the trip, rather than tourist attractions which feature only amusements and entertainment. It is urged that attendance at conservative churches along the way and visits with Christian friends and relatives be part of the trip.[34]

At Home and Work

"The Christian home is the nearest situation to heaven on earth," according to an Eastern Pennsylvania Mennonite writer.[35] The same group tells how this goal might be accomplished, "We earnestly admonish all our brethren and sisters upon whom rests the responsibility of making the Christian home what it ought to be, to do all in their power to make their homes models in simplicity and cleanliness, in true Christian piety, in love, in uplifting influence, in devotion to the cause of Christ and the church, headquarters for godly influences, training schools for God where children are brought up in the nurture and admonition of the Lord, where boys and girls grow up to be faithful men and women for the Lord and faithful workers in the church."[36]

Conservative Mennonites strongly believe that it is impossible to properly care for and train children when both parents work full-time away from home. The traditional role of motherhood is upheld, and the God-endowed qualities of mothers are seen as best suited for homemaking. Married women, especially those with young children, normally do not work away from home. Children are regarded as God's greatest gift to the home.[37] "Christian parents welcome children, and endeavor to faithfully train them in a God-fearing manner to work together for the welfare of each other and those around them,"[38] writes one conservative Mennonite.

A family devotional time is an integral part of conservative Mennonite life. "When devotional life and the family altar are pushed out of his schedule, one is busier than God ever intended him to be," admonishes the Pilgrim Mennonite Conference.[39] It is also expected that each individual will have a time of personal prayer and Bible study. It would be unthinkable to eat without offering a prayer of thanks. Conservative Mennonites normally pray audibly and spontaneously.

While many conservative Mennonites are engaged in various kinds of agricultural occupations, many others are not farmers. One may find a great number of vocations represented (builders, electricians, plumbers, welders, printers, mechanics, furniture makers), but some jobs are definitely off limits. Any work associated in any way with defense, law enforcement, alcoholic beverages, tobacco, television, pornography, or other obviously objectionable occupa-

Social activities involving the family and the church are the primary leisure-time activities of conservative Mennonites. Most entertainment and sports are seen as frivolous if not harmful.

tions is strictly out of the question. Any government related work is usually forbidden. Jobs that keep a man away from home for long periods of time, and those that require a uniform or wearing other than the regulation plain clothing are discouraged. Since education beyond high school is cautioned against, there are few high level professionals among conservative Mennonites.

Television

The conservative Mennonite attitude toward television is summed up in a statement contained in the *Rules and Discipline of the Mid-Atlantic Mennonite Fellowship*, "Television is a modern means of communication with great potential in molding the thinking and the character of both young and old. While television is used sometimes to promote worthy causes, yet by far the greater part of what it brings into the home is entertainment, propaganda, and commercials. Television programs are often destructive to the spirtual life and undermine the principles of separation from the world, the precepts of Christian morality, the proper respect for human life, and the sanctity of marriage and the Chritian home.

"We believe that the evil influence of television greatly outweighs that which is good. For the spiritual protection, blessing, and testimony of the Church, we ask the brotherhood to abstain from the use and ownership of television. Members who are responsible for the use and ownership of telvision forfeit their membership."

Radio

While nearly all conservative Mennonites have absolutely forbidden television, radio has been another matter. By the time of the first Conservative Mennonite Movement withdrawals in the late 1950s, radios had been permitted, or at least tolerated, in many Mennonite Church conferences for many years. While many conservative groups forbad radios from their beginnings, others determined to gradually get rid of them. The latter was the case with the Eastern Pennsylvania Mennonite Church which began in 1968 and did not make radios a test of membership until 1973. About half of the Conservative Mennonite Movement groups do permit radios, but all caution against misusing the devices. *The Rules and Discipline of the Southeastern Mennonite Conference* states, "We believe that much of radio programming is dominated by the spirit of the world and exerts a damaging influence upon the spiritual life of the home. Therefore we commend and encourage those who refrain from its ownership and use for the spiritual safeguard of their homes. We caution users against indiscriminate use of the radio for both secular and religious broadcasts. Furthermore, we lay the responsibility upon users for control to maintain Christian standards and the Christian atmosphere in the home." The tolerance of radios has been an important division line among conservative Mennonites, although there are some instances in which non-radio groups fellowship with radio users.[40]

Most conservative Mennonite groups do allow tape players, although the kinds of tapes played are often restricted to a cappella singing and sermons. The Washington-Franklin Conference does not allow tape players and does not permit church services to be recorded. According to the church discipline of this group, "To minimize the temptation to criticize or disrespect sacred things, sermons or other religious activities shall not be mechanically recorded."[41]

Attendance at film and live drama theaters is another activity prohibited by the great majority of conservative Mennonites. Many groups also forbid any kind of dramatic presentations at school or youth activities much less at church. Activities purely for entertainment or pleasure seeking are strongly curbed. The Eastern Pennsylvania Mennonites are not to take part in "fairs, parades, circuses, moving picture shows, theatres, drama, bathing resorts, organized contesting ball teams, dancing, card parties, races, various forms of gambling, scavenger hunts, mystery suppers, hayrides and such like."[42]

The Woman's Head Covering

The woman's head covering is regarded as a biblical ordinance and not just another item of clothing. This practice is based on the New Testament scripture, I Corinthians 11:1-16 especially verses 3 and 5, ". . . the head of every man is Christ; and the head of the woman is the man. . . every woman that prayeth or prophesieth with her head uncovered dishonoreth her head. . . "

Many writings have been made among conservative Mennonites supporting the "Christian woman's veiling." The *Statement of Standards of the Mennonite Christian Brotherhood* summarizes the basic belief on this matter, "The Woman's Veil is a veil of religious significance and is not

Conservative Mennonites consider the woman's head covering an important Christian symbol which is to be worn consistently over uncut hair. Tie strings on coverings are required in some groups, discouraged in others, and optional in still others (like the Eastern Pennsylvania Mennonite Church to which the people in this picture belong). In some conservative Mennonite groups, men are encouraged to wear plain hats. Nearly all conservative Mennonite men are clean shaven, but in some churches, especially those of Amish background, a few men do wear beards.

a weather garb. It signifies the principles of headship. The Scripture teaches that the veil should be a covering for the head and suggests that it be patterned after nature's covering, the hair. The Scriptures also teach that the cutting of woman's hair is contrary to the will of God. Since the principle of headship, the attitude of prayer, and the alertness to witness are to be continual on the part of Christian women, the veil should be worn at all times."

The head coverings of conservative Mennonite women usually take the form of a white net cap. The older style has a front piece with corners and tie strings. The presence of the ribbon ties is thought to keep the covering from getting too small. The women in many conservative Mennonite groups wear a rounded type covering without tie strings. The Pilgrim Mennonite Conference is very precise on covering specifications:

"The covering application to be honored at all times is a two piece type of sufficient size so the bottom comes below the bun to the neck and the front comes forward to a position (on top of the head) in front

This illustration from the Rod and Staff tract "People Call Us Mennonites" includes most of the basic elements typical of ultra-conservative Mennonite personal appearance. For men short, neatly combed, tapered hair, clean shaven face, standing collar plain coat, no necktie, loose fitting pants, black shoes, and stockings. The dress of the boy represents the warm weather male attire of all males: long sleeved shirt with the collar buttoned and dark trousers worn with a belt. Before they become church members, which typically occurs in the early to mid-teens, boys in most groups wear conventional suitcoats with lapels, but do not wear neckties. The woman wears a large covering over her simple combed long hair; a mid-calf length, long sleeved plain dress with an extra panel over the torso called a cape; black stockings; and plain black shoes. The little girl wears her hair in braids, no head covering or cape, and white stockings. The covering is not worn until conversion and church membership, but the cape and black stockings may be worn before this time.

of the ears. The front piece shall be at least 1½" wide. The hair shall not be cut and shall be free from current worldly arrangements which do not express a spirit of meekness and sobriety."[43]

The Rules and Discipline of the Southeastern Mennonite Conference explains why conservative Mennonite women do not cut their hair: "Regarding the hair, the Scripture teaches that a woman's cut hair is a shame to her and to her head, and that her uncut hair is her glory (I Corinthians 11:6, 14, 15). Sisters are therefore not to cut their hair. The hair should always be styled modestly so that it can be appropriately veiled."[44]

Dress

The preservation of distinctive plain dress was one of the primary reasons the Conservative Mennonite Movement arose. Conservative Mennonites continue to appreciate the value of their religious garb. The written standard of the Pilgrim Mennonite Conference gives numerous scriptural references and explains in detail the necessity of

The three young women on the left are representative of the ultra-conservative style of dress—large coverings, long dresses, and heavy black stockings. Close fitting black bonnets are also worn over the head covering for outdoor wear by many ultra-conservative women. The three women on the right are more typical of moderate-conservative Mennonites—smaller head coverings, shorter dresses, some decorative trim, and thinner stockings. The girl on the far right wears no cape on her dress. Capes are not required in some conservative groups.

"Christian Attire." Concerning modesty: "The clothes one wears reveal the desires of the inner man. Modest apparel, therefore, expresses Christian propiety and indicates the choice of a virtuous mind. This calls for one to be modestly dressed, shunning the unrestrained boldness of abbreviated and form-fitting clothing." On the subject of ornamentation: "Each time we choose to adorn ourselves we should ask the questions, 'Am I choosing these things to bring attention to God and His word or is this for my glory and pride?'" On fads and fashions: "A standard for our attire helps to avoid the changing suits of apparel which are so common in the world today, and protects against the gradual acceptance of that which would be a violation of Bible principle."[45]

John L. Stauffer succinctly summarized the conservative Mennonite attitude, "The Christian life is a supernatural life resulting from an experience with Jesus Christ. It is a life governed by the teachings of the Word of God. In every area of human experience, where a moral principle is involved, it is distinctive when compared with the life of the non-Christian. It is the will of God for the Christian that he be not conformed to this age, but transformed by the renewing of the mind (Romans 12:1, 2)."[46]

Notes

Chapter 1, pages 12-27

1. Theron F. Schlabach, *Peace, Faith, Nation: Mennonites and Amish in Nineteenth-Century America* (Scottdale, Pa.: Herald Press, 1988), 295-321.

2. John C. Wenger, "Jacob Wisler and the Old Order Mennonite Schism of 1872 in Elkhart County, Indiana," *Mennonite Quarterly Review*, 33 (Apr 1959), 130.

3. John C. Wenger, *The Yellowcreek Mennonites* (Goshen, Ind.: Yellowcreek Mennonite Church, 1985), 37.

4. John C. Wenger, *The Mennonites in Indiana and Michigan* (Scottdale, Pa.: Herald Press, 1961), 368.

5. Wenger, "Jacob Wisler (part 2)," (July 1959), 231-235.

6. John S. Umble, "Extinct Mennonite Churches in Ohio," *Mennonite Quarterly Review*, 18 (Jan, Jul, Oct 1944), 36-48, 186-192, 225-250; (Jan, Jul 1945), 41-58, 215-237; 20 (Jan 1946), 5-52.

7. Isaac R. Horst, *Closeups of the Great Awakening* (Mt. Forest, Ont.: The Author, 1985), 169.

8. Lewis J. Burkholder, *A Brief History of the Mennonites in Ontario* (Markham, Ont.: Mennonite Conference of Ontario, 1935), 198.

9. Frank H. Epp, *Mennonites in Canada, 1786-1920*, (Toronto: Macmillan of Canada, 1974), 120, 265.

10. Burkholder, *Brief History*, 197.

11. Horst, *Closeups*, 171.

12. Burkholder, *Brief History*, 199-200.

13. Amos B. Hoover, *The Jonas Martin Era* (Denver, Pa.: The Author, 1982), 148-149.

14. Lloyd M. Weiler, "Historical Overview of Weaverland Conference Origins," in *Directory of the Weaverland Conference Mennonite Churches 1995*, (Womelsdorf, Pa.: Ruth A. Wise, 1995), appendix 27,28.

15. A. Grace Wenger, *Frontiers of Faithfulness: The Story of the Groffdale Mennonite Church*, (Leola, Pa.: Groffdale Mennonite Church, 1992), 84.

16. Hoover, *Jonas Martin*, 797.

17. Wenger, *Frontiers*, 86.

18. Harry A. Brunk, *History of Mennonites in Virginia*, Vol. I, (Staunton, Va.: McClure Printing Co., 1959), 443-445.

19. Brunk, *History* I, 452-505.

20. Brunk, *History* I, 510-514.

21. Brunk, *History* I, 515-517.

22. Brunk, *History* I, 517. The number 71 includes 69 who were disowned at this time and two who had been previously disowned.

23. Harry A. Brunk, *History of Mennonites in Virginia*, Vol. II, (Verona, Va.: McClure Printing Co, 1972), 517.

24. Brunk, *History* II, 517-519.

25. Hoover, *Jonas Martin*, 392.

26. John C. Wenger, *History of the Mennonites of the Franconia Conference*, (Telford, Pa.: Franconia Mennonite Historical Society, 1937), 274-275.

Chapter 2, pages 28-69

1. Hoover, *Jonas Martin*, 812-813.

2. Joseph S. Shirk and Ezra S. Zimmerman, *Records of the Old Order Mennonites from 1750 to 1963*, (New Holland and Ephrata, Pa.: The Authors, [1963]), 6.

3. Wenger, *Indiana and Michigan*, 371-372.

4. Brunk, History II, 520-521.

5. "School Directory," Blackboard Bulletin (Nov. 1993), 21-25.

6. Isaac R. Horst, Up the Conestogo, (Mt. Forest, Ont.: The Author, 1979), 326-327.

7. "School Directory," 23,24.

8. "School Directory," 22.

Chapter 3, pages 70-87

1. Amos B. Hoover, "Historical Sketches of the Weaverland Conference Congregations," in Directory of the Weaverland Conference Mennonite Churches 1990 (Womelsdorf, Pa.: Ruth A. Wise, 1990), Appendix 28.

2. Hoover, Historical Sketches, 17.

3. "List of Cars Not Acceptable in the Vehicle Aid Plan for Jan. 1994," Home Messenger (March 1994), insert.

4. Homer K. Luttringer, The Innovators: The New Holland Story, (Lancaster, Pa.: The Author, 1990), 13-19, 26-30.

New Holland Machine had been founded by Abe Zimmerman, an ex-Mennonite whose father was involved in the pulpit removing incident at Lichty's Mennonite Church described in Chapter 1.

Chapter 4, pages 88-100

1. Jacob W. Stauffer, A Chronicle of History Booklet About the So-Called Mennonite Church, trans. Amos B. Hoover (1855; reprint Lancaster, Pa.: Lancaster Mennonite Historical Society, 1992). The material in this chapter relating to the beginning of the Stauffer Mennonite Church is largely based on this book.

2. Stauffer, Chronicle, 90.

3. Stauffer, Chronicle, 89.

4. Stauffer, Chronicle, 123-124.

5. Stauffer, Chronicle, 178.

6. Record of Members of the Stauffer Mennonite Church at the Present Time, 1977, (Gordonville, Pa.: Gordonville Print Shop, 1977).

7. Louella Stauffer, Record of Members of the Stauffer Mennonite Church at the Present Time, 1990, (Gordonville, Pa.: Gordonville Print Shop, 1990).

8. Hoover, Jonas Martin, 506-509.

9. Enos Stauffer, Die Briefe an David Stauffer, (Gordonville, Pa.: Gordonville Print Shop, 1990), 733.

10. The material in this chart was based on the following sources:

Hoover, Jonas Martin, 50.

Enos E. Stauffer, Uncle Aaron Stauffer's Diary 1947-1956, (Port Trevorton, Pa.: 1995).

Enos E. Stauffer, "Snyder County Old Order Mennonite Ministers' List 1845-." Historical Center Echoes 16 (January 1993): 7-9.

Personal correspondence with Amos B. Hoover and Enos E. Stauffer.

Chapter 5, pages 105-119

1. Wilmer J. Eshleman, A History of the Reformed Mennonite Church, (Lancaster, Pa.: Graphic Crafts, 1969), 12.

2. Daniel Musser, The Reformed Mennonite Church, 2nd ed. (Lancaster, Pa.: Inquirer Publishing and Printing, 1878). The material in this chapter on the beginnings of the Reformed Mennonite Church is largely based on information con- tained in this book.

3. The Unity and Purity of the Church, (Lancaster, Pa.: The Reformed Mennonite Church, 1970), 10.

4. The Reformed Mennonites, (Lancaster, Pa.: The Reformed Mennonite Church, 1974), 8.

5. Lancaster Sunday News, 2 May 1976.

6. *Carlisle Evening Sentinel*, 5 Dec. 1983.

7. A. Hunter Rineer, *The Churches and Cemeteries of Lancaster County*, (Lancaster, Pa.: Lancaster County Historical Society, 1993), 14.

8. *Religious Bodies: 1906, Part II*, (Washington: Government Printing Office, 1910), 415-416.

9. Epp, *Mennonites in Canada, 1786-1920*, 321.

10. *Mennonite Yearbook*, 1956, 122.

11. Rineer, *Churches*, 14.

12. Cornelius J. Dyck and Dennis D. Martin eds., *Mennonite Encyclopedia Vol. V*, (Scottdale, Pa.: 1990), 753.

13. Eugene Kraybill, *700 Churches*, (Lancaster, Pa.: 1985), 19.

14. Dyck, *Mennonite Encyclopedia V*, 753.

15. *Christianity Defined*, (Lancaster, Pa.: Reformed Mennonite Church, 1958), 143.

16. Levi Miller, "Daniel Musser and Leo Tolstoy," *Mennonite Historical Bulletin*, LIV (Apr. 1993), 1-7.

17. Martin E. Ressler, *An Annotated Bibliography of Mennonite Hymnals and Songbooks 1742-1986*. (Gordonville, Pa.: Gordonville Print Shop, 1987), 83-87.

Chapter 6, pages 122-136

1. S. Duane Kauffman, *Mifflin County Amish and Mennonite Story*. Belleville, Pa.: Mifflin County Mennonite Historical Society, 1991), 121-122.

2. *Mennonite Yearbook*, 1921 and 1961.

3. Ivan J. Miller, *History of the Conservative Mennonite Conference*, (Grantsville, Md.: The Author, 1985), 163.

4. Elmer S. Yoder and Jewel Showalter, *We Beheld His Glory*, (Irwin, Ohio: Rosedale Bible Institute, 1992).

5. *Statement on Inter-Mennonite Relationships* (Irwin, Ohio: Conservative Mennonite Conference, 1992).

Chapter 7, pages 137-158

1. 'Mennonite General Conference," *Gospel Herald*, (November 24, 1944), 676-677.

2. Beulah S. Hostetler, *American Mennonites and Protestant Movements*, (Scottdale, Pa.: Herald Press, 1987), 267.

3. [J. Irvin Lehman], "General Conference 1953," *The Sword and Trumpet*, (Fourth Quarter, 1953), 5.

4. J. Ward Shank, "Impressions During 1959 General Conference," *Sword and Trumpet*, (Third Quarter, 1959), 33.

5. "Mass Media," *Mennonite Encyclopedia Vol. V*, 545.

Chapter 8, pages 159-198

1. *The Conservative Mennonite Fellowship*, (Hartville, Ohio.: Fellowship Messenger, 1968), 3,4.

2. *Mennonite Yearbook*, 1967, 90-91.

3. *Conservative Mennonite Fellowship*, 32.

4. *Conservative Mennonite Fellowship*, 33-35.

5. Dorcas Hoover, *Awaiting the Dawn*, (Harrisonburg, Va.: Christian Light Publications, 1992).

6. Hoover, *Awaiting*, 121-122.

7. *Mennonite Yearbook*, 1996, 112.

8. Dennis Baer, "A Brief History and a Challenge Part 2," *Christian Contender*, (July 1990), 10.

9. Baer, "History Part 3," (August 1990), 6.

10. Baer, "History Part 3," (August 1990), 7.

11. *Mennonite Yearbook*, 1996, 112.

12. Robert B. Graber, "An Amiable

Mennonite Schism," *Pennsylvania Mennonite Heritage* 7 (October 1984), 6.

13. Graber, "Amiable Mennonite Schism," 6.

14. Graber, "Amiable Mennonite Schism," 7.

15. Graber, "Amiable Mennonite Schism," 8.

16. *Mennonite Yearbook*, 1970, 85.

17. 1995 *Directory of the Eastern Pennsylvania Mennonite Church and Related Areas*, (Ephrata, Pa.: Publication Board of the Eastern Pennsylvania Mennonite Church, 1995).

18. "Our Guatemala Mission Interests," *The Eastern Mennonite Testimony*, (January 1972), 4.

19. Larry Weaver, "Reflections on Mission Work in Guatemala," *The Eastern Mennonite Testimony* (January 1993), 10.

20. Floyd K. Martin, "Decker Lake Mennonite Church History," *The Eastern Mennonite Testimony* (April 1983), 56.

21. David N. Wadel, "South of the Equator," *The Eastern Mennonite Testimony* (April 1982), 46.

22. Clarence E. Martin, "Time Line of the Development of the Bahamas Church," *The Eastern Mennonite Testimony* (May 1994), 8,9.

23. Clarence E. Martin, "Literature Evangelism Committee Report," *The Eastern Mennonite Testimony* (June 1991), 10.

24. David G. Weaver, "Publication Board Report," *The Eastern Mennonite Testimony* (January 1993), 11.

25. 1995 *Directory of the Eastern Pennsylvania Mennonite Church*, 35.

26. *Statement of Christian Doctrine and Rules and Discipline of the Eastern Pennsylvania Church and Related Areas* 1993, (n.p. [1993]), 13.

27. *Directory of County Line,* Woodlawn, Maple Hill, Salem Mennonite *Churches* 1995, (n.p. [1995]).

28. "Minutes of the Conferring Fellowship Meeting," *The Eastern Mennonite Testimony* (May 1992), 6.

29. Eastern Pennsylvania Mennonite Church Bishops, "Statement of Proceedings Regarding Brother Homer Bomberger's Status in the Eastern Pennsylvania Mennonite Church," *The Eastern Mennonite Testimony* (May 1972), 58,59.

"Announcements," *The Eastern Mennonite Testimony* (June 1972), 62.

30. *Mennonite Yearbook*, 1975, 66-67.

31. Fred L. Kniss, "Disquiet in the Land" (Ph.D. diss., University of Chicago, 1992), 117,118.

32. *Mennonite Yearbook*, 1995, 122.

33. Hope Lind, *Apart and Together,* (Scottdale, Pa.: Herald Press, 1990) 96, 112.

34. Lind, *Apart,* 125.

35. Lind, *Apart,* 126-127.

36. Lind, *Apart,* 126.

37. *Bible Mennonite Fellowship, Confession of Faith, Discipline, Constitution,* (n.p. 1982), 1.

38. *Bible Mennonite,* 29.

39. *The Berea Declaration* [Berea, Ohio, 1984].

40. *Evangelical Anabaptist Fellowship: Our Purpose, Program, Declaration and Vision,* (Harrisonburg, Va.: Evangelical Anabaptist Fellowship, n.d.)

41. *Introducing Evangelical Anabaptist Fellowship* (Harrisonburg, Va.: Evangelical Anabaptist Fellowship, n.d.)

42. *Yearbook Church of God in Christ, Mennonite* 1995.

Chapter 9, pages 199-232

1. Daniel Kauffman, *Doctrines of the Bible*, (Scottdale, Pa.: Mennonite

Publishing House, 1928), 17.

2. *Statement of Faith of the Southeastern Mennonite Conference*, (n.p. 1991), 29.

3. John Coblentz, *Are Written Standards for the Church?* (Harrisonburg, Va.: Christian Light Publications, 1991) The material in the above two paragaraphs are largely based on this source.

4. *Statement of Faith*, 14, 15.

5. *Statement of Faith*, 15.

6. *Statement of Christian Doctrine*, 13.

7. *Statement of Christian Doctrine*, 13.

8. John Coblentz and Merna Shank, *Proclaiming God's Truth*, (Harrisonburg, Va.: Christian Light Publications, 1994), various pages.

9. David G. Weaver, "Publication Board General Report." *The Eastern Mennonite Testimony*, (January 1993), 11.

10. "Mennonites, Who They Are What They Believe," Christian Light Publications tract. Scripture references Matthew 28:19, 20 and James 2: 15, 16.

11. *Statement of Christian Doctrine*, Scriptural references: I Timothy 2:1-3, Romans 13:1-5, Titus 3:1.

12. Ralph Shank, *The Christian's Relation to the State*, (Crockett, Ky.: Rod and Staff Publishers, n.d.), 5.

13. Acts 5:29

14. John 18:36

15. John 18:36

16. Matthew 26:52

17. Matthew 5:44

18. Matthew 5:39

19. *Statement of Christian Doctrine*, 19.

20. Aaron M. Shank, *Studies in the Doctrine of Nonresistance*, (Lititz, Pa.: Publication Board of The Eastern Pennsylvania Mennonite Church, 1989), 27.

21. Shank, *The Christian's Relation*.

22. Shank, *Studies*.

23. Matthew 5:33-37 and James 5:12.

24. *Neglected, Rejected and Forgotten Truths*, (Crockett, Ky.: Rod and Staff Publishers, 1992).

25. Jesse Neuenschwander, "Protecting Our Young People," *Eastern Mennonite Testimony* (Jan 1995), 3.

26. "Agreement Among the Bishops on How We View Play Activities Among Church Members," unpublished paper.

27. *Decrees for to Keep for the Pilgrim Mennonite Conference of the Church of Jesus Christ 1992*, (n.p. [1992]), 34.

28. *The Christian Wedding*, (Dayton, Va.: The Southeastern Mennonite Conference, 1977)

29. *Statement of Faith*, 28. Scripture references cited: Matthew 5:31,32; Luke 16:18; I Corinthians 7:10-15; Romans 7:1-3.

30. *Preparing for Christian Weddings and Godly Homes*, (Lititz, Pa.: Eastern Mennonite Publications, 1989) 11-17 (source for this paragraph).

31. *Preparing for Christian Weddings*, 61.

32. *The Christian Wedding*.

33. *The Christian Wedding*.

34. *Preparing for Christian Weddings*.

35. Sidney M. Carpenter, "Christian Simplicity in Home Life," *The Eastern Mennonite Testimony*, (Feb. 1978), 17.

36. *Statement of Christian Doctrine*, 30.

37. *Homemaking an Honorable Role* (Crockett, Ky.: Rod and Staff Publishers, 1993).

38. Mark Carpenter, "Parents Communicating Practical Separation," *The Eastern Mennonite Testimony*, (June 1994), 4.

39. *Decrees for to Keep*, 11.

40. *Statement of Faith*, 32-33.

41. *Doctrinal Statement and Discipline of the Washington Co., Md. and Franklin*

Co., Pa. Mennonite Church Conference,
(n.p., 1994).

    42. *Statement of Christian Doctrine*, 20.

    43. *Decrees for to Keep*, 24.

    44. *Statement of Faith*, 27.

    45. *Decrees for to Keep*, 26-31.

    46. John L. Stauffer, *Why Should Christians Wear Distinctive Attire?* (Crockett, Ky.: Rod and Staff Publishers, n.d.), 2.

Bibliography

"Agreement Among the Bishops on How We View Play Activities Among Church Members," [Eastern Pennsylvania Mennonite Church], n.d. unpublished paper.

Articles of Faith, Rules and Discipline, Constitution and By-Laws of the Mid-Atlantic Mennonite Fellowship, n.p., 1987.

Baer, Dennis. "A Brief History and a Challenge." *The Christian Contender* 30 (June, July, August, September 1990).

Baer, Mervin. *Changing Church Patterns and Their Ultimate Result.* Crockett, Ky.: Rod and Staff Publishers, 1963.

Baer, Mervin. *Come Out, My People!* Crockett, Ky.: Rod and Staff Publishers, n.d.

Bender, Harold S. *The Anabaptist Vision.* Scottdale, Pa.: Herald Press, 1944.

Bender, Harold S., et. al., *John Horsch Memorial Papers.* Scottdale, Pa.: Mennonite Publishing House, 1947.

Bender, Harold S., and C. Henry Smith, eds. Vol. 1-4; Cornelius J. Dyck and Dennis D. Martin, eds. Vol. 5. *The Mennonite Encyclopedia.* Scottdale, Pa.: Mennonite Publishing House, Vol. 1-4, 1955-1959, Vol. 5, 1990.

Benowitz, Jean-Paul. "Community in Conflict: The Structure of the Old Order Mennonite Church in Virginia." Masters thesis, Millersville University, 1993.

Benowitz, Jean-Paul. "The Old Order Mennonite Division of 1893: An Interpretation." *Pennsylvania Mennonite Heritage* 16 (October 1993): 14-17.

Berry, Roger and Lloyd Hartzler. *Separation and Nonconformity.* Harrisonburg, Va.: Christian Light Publications, 1986.

Bible Mennonite Fellowship Confession of Faith, Discipline, Constitution. 1982.

A Brief Statement of Bible Doctrine, 18 Articles of Faith. Crockett, Ky.: Rod and Staff Publishers, 1980.

Brunk, George R. II. *A Crisis Among Mennonites - In Education - In Publication.* Harrisonburg, Va.: The Sword and Trumpet, 1983.

Brunk, Harry Anthony. *History of Mennonites in Virginia.* Vol. I 1727-1900, Vol. II 1900-1960. Staunton, Va.: McClure Printing Company, 1959 and 1972.

Building Christian Homes. Lititz, Pa.: Eastern Mennonite Publications, 1991.

Burkholder, Lewis J. *A Brief History of the Mennonites in Ontario.* Mennonite Conference of Ontario, 1935.

The Christian Wedding. Southeastern Mennonite Conference, 1977.

Christianity Defined. Lancaster, Pa.: Reformed Mennonite Church, 1958.

Coblentz, John. *Are Written Standards for the Church?* Harrisonburg, Va.: Christian Light Publications, 1991.

Coblentz, John, *Merna Shank and Others Proclaiming God's Truth: The First 25 Years at Christian Light Publications 1969-1994.* Harrisonburg, Va.: Christian Light Publications, 1994.

Coffman, Barbara R. *His Name Was*

John: The Life Story of an Early
Mennonite Leader [John Coffman].
Scottdale, Pa.: Herald Press,
1964.

Confession of Faith and Practice, n.p.:
[Charity Christian Fellowship],
1993.

The Conservative Mennonite Fellowship: A
Brief Account of the First Ten Years
1957-1966. Hartville, Ohio: The
Fellowship Messenger, 1968.

Conservative Mennonite Statement of
Theology. Irwin, Ohio:
Conservative Mennonite
Conference, 1991.

Constitution and Faith and Practice of the
Conservative Mennonite Church of
Ontario, n.p., 1989.

Decrees for to Keep for the Pilgrim
Mennonite Conference of the Church of
Jesus Christ, n.p., 1992.

Directory of County Line, Woodlawn,
Maple Hill, Salem Mennonite
Churches 1995, n.p. [1995].

Directory of the Eastern Pennsylvania
Mennonite Church. Ephrata, Pa.:
Publication Board of the Eastern
Pennsylvania Mennonite Church,
1969-.

Doctrinal Statement and Discipline of the
Cumberland Valley Mennonite
Church, n.p., 1992.

Doctrinal Statement and Discipline of the
Washington Co., Md., and Franklin
Co., Pa., Mennonite Church
Conference. 1994.

Dyck, Cornelius J. An Introduction to
Mennonite History. Scottdale, Pa.:
Herald Press, 1993.

Eastern Mennonite Testimony. 1969- .
Ephrata, Pa.: Eastern Mennonite
Publications.

Ebersole, Stephen. People Call Us
Mennonites. Crockett, Ky.: Rod and
Staff Publishers, 1988.

Epp, Frank H. Mennonites in Canada,
1786-1920: The History of a Separate

People. Toronto: Macmillan of
Canada, 1974.

Epp, Frank H. Mennonites in Canada,
1920-1940: A People's Struggle for
Survival. Scottdale, Pa.: Herald
Press, 1982.

Eshleman, Wilmer J. A History of the
Reformed Mennonite Church.
Lancaster, Pa.: Graphic Crafts,
1969.

Evangelical Anabaptist Fellowship: Our
Purpose, Program, Declaration and
Vision, Harrisonburg, Va.:
Evangelical Anabaptist
Fellowship, n.d.

Fretz, J. Winfield. "The Old Order
Mennonites in Ontario."
Pennsylvania Mennonite Heritage 3
(January 1980): 2-10.

Fretz, J. Winfield. The Waterloo
Mennonites. Waterloo, Ontario:
Wilfrid Laurier University Press
for Conrad Grebel College, 1989.

Gates, Helen Kolb; John Funk Kolb;
J. Clemens Kolb; Constance Kolb
Sykes. Bless The Lord O My Soul: A
Biography of Bishop John Fretz Funk.
Scottdale, Pa.: Herald Press,
1964.

Gingerich, Alice K. Life and Times of
Daniel Kauffman. Scottdale, Pa.:
Herald Press, 1954.

Goering, James A. Nonresistance or
Pacifism - Which? Harrisonburg,
Va.: Christian Light Publications,
1974.

Graber, Robert B. "An Amiable
Mennonite Schism: The Origin of
the Eastern Pennsylvania
Mennonite Church." Pennsylvania
Mennonite Heritage 7 (October
1984): 2-10.

Graber, Robert B. "The Sociocultural
Differentiation of a Religious
Sect." Ph.D. diss., University of
Wisconsin-Milwaukee, 1979.

Hartzler, Lloyd. Personal Appearance in

the Light of God's Word.
Harrisonburg, Va.: Christian Light
Publications, n.d.

Homemaking - an Honorable Role.
Crockett, Ky.: Rod and Staff
Publishers, 1993.

Hoover, Amos B. "Historical
Sketches of the Weaverland
Conference Mennonite
Congregations." In Directory of
the Weaverland Conference
Mennonite Churches, Ruth Ann
Wise and Lucille H. Martin. 1990.

Hoover, Amos B. *The Jonas Martin Era.*
Denver, Pa.: Amos B. Hoover,
1982.

Hoover, Amos B. "The Old Order
Mennonites." In *Mennonite World
Handbook.* edited by Paul N.
Kraybill. Lombard, Illinois:
Mennonite World Conference,
1978.

Hoover, Amos B. "A Tear for Jonas
Martin: Old Order Mennonite
Origins in Lancaster County."
Pennsylvania Folklife 33 (Winter
1983/84): 90-94.

Hoover, Dorcas. *Awaiting the Dawn.*
Harrisonburg, Va.: Christian Light
Publications, 1992.

Hoover, John David. "An Old Order
Mennonite Wedding Ceremony
in Pennsylvania." *Pennsylvania
Mennonite Heritage* 13 (July 1990):
11.

Horsch, John. *The Mennonite Church
and Modernism.* Scottdale, Pa.:
Mennonite Publishing House,
1924.

Horsch, John. *Mennonites in Europe.*
Scottdale, Pa.: Mennonite
Publishing House, 1942.

Horsch, John. *Modern Religious
Liberalism.* Scottdale, Pa.:
Mennonite Publishing House,
1924.

Horsch, John. *The Principle of

*Nonresistance As Held by the
Mennonite Church.* Scottdale, Pa.:
Mennonite Publishing House,
1927.

Horsch, John. *Worldly Conformity in
Dress.* Scottdale, Pa.: Mennonite
Publishing House, [1925].

Horst, Isaac R. *Close Ups of the Great
Awakening.* Mt. Forest, Ont.: Isaac
R. Horst, 1985.

Horst, Isaac R. *Separate and Peculiar.*
[Mt. Forest, Ont.]: Isaac R. Horst,
1979.

Horst, Isaac R. *Up the Conestogo.* Mt.
Forest, Ont.: Isaac R. Horst, 1979.

Horst, Isaac R. *Why Grossdaudy?* Mt.
Forest, Ont.: Isaac R. Horst, 1985.

Horst, Mary Ann. *My Old Order
Mennonite Heritage.* Kitchener,
Ont.: Pennsylvania Dutch Crafts
and Local Books, 1992.

Horst, Melvin G. *Distinctive Attire for
Christians.* Crockett, Ky.: Rod and
Staff Publishers, 1971.

Hurst, Emma. *Moses G. Horning and
the Old Order Divisions in
Pennsylvania.* [Harrisonburg, Va.]:
Eastern Mennonite College,
1960.

Hostetler, Beulah Stauffer. *American
Mennonites and Protestant
Movements.* Scottdale, Pa.: Herald
Press, 1987.

Huber, Clarence. *The Relationship of
Church and State.* Crockett, Ky.:
Rod and Staff Publishers, n.d.

Huber, Harold. *With Eyes of Faith*: A
*History of Greenwood Mennonite
Church, Greenwood, Delaware* 1914-
1974. Greenwood, Del.: The
Country Rest Home and Mr. and
Mrs. Laban L. Swartzentruber,
1974.

*Introducing Evangelical Anabaptist
Fellowship.* Harrisonburg, Va.:
Evangelical Anabaptist
Fellowship, n.d.

Jentsch, Theodore Werner. *Mennonite Americans: A Study of a Religious Subculture From a Sociological Perspective*. Ph.D. diss., University of South Africa, 1973.

Jentsch, Theodore Werner. "Education, Occupation and Economics Among Old Order Mennonites of the East Penn Valley." *Pennsylvania Folklife* 24 (Spring 1975): 24-35.

Jentsch, Theodore Werner. "Old Order Mennonite Family Life in the East Penn Valley." *Pennsylvania Folklife* 24 (Fall 1974): 18-27.

Juhnke, James C. *Vision, Doctrine, War: Mennonite Identity and Organization in America 1890-1930. The Mennonite Experience in America, Volume 3*. Scottdale, Pa.: Herald Press, 1989.

Kauffman, Daniel, ed. *Doctrines of the Bible*. Scottdale, Pa.: Mennonite Publishing House, 1928.

Kauffman, Daniel. *The Mennonite Church and Current Issues*. Scottdale, Pa.: Mennonite Publishing House, 1923.

Kauffman, Daniel. *1,000 Questions and Answers on Points of Christian Doctrine*. Scottdale, Pa.: Mennonite Publishing House, 1908.

Kauffman, S. Duane. *Mifflin County Amish and Mennonite Story*. Belleville, Pa.: Mifflin County Mennonite Historical Society, 1991.

Kaylor, Steven L. "The Old Order Mennonite Meetinghouses of Lancaster County, Pennsylvania," *Historic Schaefferstown Record* 21 (July, 1987): 47-68.

Kniss, Fred Lamar. *Disquiet in the Land: Conflict Over Ideas and Symbols Among American Mennonites, 1870-*

1985. University of Chicago, Ph.D. 1992.

Kniss, Fred Lamar. "Intra-denominational Ideological Conflict: The Fellowship of Concerned Mennonites." Graduate Paper, Department of Sociology, University of Chicago, 1986.

Kraybill, Eugene. *700 Churches*. Lancaster, Pennsylvania: *Intelligencer Journal*, 1985.

Kropf, Wilbur. *The Plural Ministry*. Crockett, Ky.: Rod and Staff Publishers, 1970.

Landis, Paul M. *Must We Accept the Radio and TV?* Crockett, Ky.: Rod and Staff Publishers, n.d.

Leaders and Institutions of the Southeastern Mennonite Conference. [Southeastern Mennonite Conference, ca. 1981.]

Lehman, Daniel R. *Mennonites of the Washington County, Maryland and Franklin County, Pennsylvania Conference*. Lititz, Pa.: Eastern Mennonite Publications, 1990.

Lehman, Jacob S. *The Church of Christ and Its Characteristics of Unity, Peace and Purity*. Lancaster, Pa.: Reformed Mennonite Church, 1964.

Leid, Noah W. *History of the Bowmansville Mennonites and Related Congregations, Old Order Groups*. East Earl, Pa.: 1976.

Lind, Hope Kauffman. *Apart and Together: Mennonites in Oregon and Neighboring States 1876-1976*. Scottdale, Pa.: Herald Press, 1990.

Luttringer, Homer K. *The Innovators: The New Holland Story*. Lancaster, Pa.: The Author, 1990.

MacMaster, Richard K. *Land, Piety, Peoplehood: The Establishment of Mennonite Communities in America 1683-1790. The Mennonite*

Experience in America, Volume 1. Scottdale, Pa.: Herald Press, 1985.

Martin, Ezra. *Mennonite Settlement, May City, Iowa, 1887-1915.* Ephrata, Pa.: Ezra Martin, 1983.

Martin, Raymond S. and Elizabeth S. Martin. *Bishop Jonas Martin: His Life and Genealogy.* Baltimore: Gateway Press, 1985.

McGrath, William. *Did God Lose the Election?* Crockett, Ky.: Rod and Staff Publishers, n.d.

Mennonite Christian Brotherhood Statement of Standards. Ephrata, Pa.: Grace Press, 1990.

Mennonite Confession of Faith. Crockett, Ky.: Rod and Staff Publishers, 1965.

Mennonite Confession of Faith, Adopted by Mennonite General Conference August 22, 1963. Scottdale, Pa.: Herald Press, 1963.

Mennonite Yearbook. Currently published by Scottdale, Pa.: Mennonite Publishing House, 1905- .

The Mennonites. Crockett, Ky.: Rod and Staff Publishers, 1972.

Mennonites: Who They Are, What They Believe. Harrisonburg, Va.: Christian Light Publications, n.d.

Midwest Mennonite Fellowship Constitution, Bible School Policy, Nonresistance Statement. 1980.

Miller, Ivan J. *History of the Conservative Mennonite Conference 1910-1985.* Grantsville, Maryland: Ivan J. and Della Miller, 1985.

Miller, Levi. "Daniel Musser and Leo Tolstoy," *Mennonite Historical Bulletin,* LIV (Apr. 1993), 1-7.

Musser, Daniel. *The Reformed Mennonite Church: Its Rise and Progress With Its Principles and Doctrines.* 2nd ed. Lancaster, Pa.: Inquirer Printing and Publishing Co., 1878.

Neglected, Rejected and Forgotten Truths. Crockett, Ky.: Rod and Staff Publishers, 1972.

Nolt, Steven M. "Church Discipline in the Lancaster Mennonite Conference: The Printed Rules and Discipline, 1881-1968." *Pennsylvania Mennonite Heritage* 15 (October 1992): 2-16.

Our Congregation Prepares for an Ordination. Bishop Board of Lancaster Conference, 1959. Reprint. Farmington, New Mexico: Lamp and Light Publishers, 1983.

Publication Board of the Eastern Pennsylvania Mennonite Church. *Instructions for Christian Living and Church Membership.* Lititz, Pa.: Eastern Mennonite Publications, 1984.

Publication Board of the Eastern Pennsylvania Mennonite Church. *Preparing for Christian Weddings and Godly Homes.* Lititz, Pa.: Eastern Mennonite Publications, 1989.

Publication Board of the Eastern Pennsylvania Mennonite Church. *The Swiss Anabaptists: A Brief Summary of Their History and Beliefs.* Ephrata, Pa.: Eastern Mennonite Publications, 1990.

The Reformed Mennonites: Who They Are and What They Believe. Lancaster, Pa.: The Reformed Mennonite Church, 1974.

Record of Members of the Stauffer Mennonite Church at the Present Time, 1977. Gordonville, Pa.: Gordonville Print Shop, 1977.

Reimer, Margaret Loewen. *One Quilt Many Pieces: A Reference Guide to Mennonite Groups in Canada.* Waterloo, Ont.: Mennonite Publishing Service, 1983.

Religious Bodies: 1906. Washington: Government Printing Office, 1910.

The Responsibility of the Church to Her Youth. Southeastern Mennonite Conference, 1981.

Ressler, Martin E. *An Annotated Bibliography of Mennonite Hymnals and Songbooks 1742-1986.* Gordonville, Pa., 1987.

Richard, Kent E. *Fairmount Homes: A 25th Anniversary History.* Ephrata, Pa.: Fairmount Homes, 1993.

Rineer, A. Hunter. *The Churches and Cemeteries of Lancaster County: A Complete Guide.* Lancaster, Pa.: Lancaster County Historical Society, 1993.

Ruth, John L. *Maintaining the Right Fellowship: A Narrative Account of Life in the Oldest Mennonite Community in North America.* Scottdale, Pa.: Herald Press, 1984.

Ruth, Merle. *The Significance of the Christian Woman's Veiling.* Crockett, Ky.: Rod and Staff Publishers, 1980.

Schlabach, Theron F. *Gospel Versus Gospel: Mission and the Mennonite Church.* Scottdale, Pa.: Herald Press, 1980.

Schlabach, Theron F. *Peace, Faith, Nation: Mennonites and Amish in Nineteenth-Century America. The Mennonite Experience in America, Volume 2.* Scottdale, Pa.: Herald Press, 1988.

"School Directory," *Blackboard Bulletin* (Nov. 1993), 21-25.

Scott, Stephen. *The Amish Wedding and Other Special Occasions of the Old Order Communities.* Intercourse, Pa.: Good Books, 1988.

Scott, Stephen. *Plain Buggies: Amish, Mennonite, and Brethren Horse-Drawn Transportation.* Intercourse, Pa.: Good Books, 1981.

Scott, Stephen. *Why Do They Dress That Way?* Intercourse, Pa.: Good Books, 1986.

Scott, Stephen and Kenneth Pellman. *Living Without Electricity.* Intercourse, Pa.: Good Books, 1990.

Shertzer, Yvonne. *Silver Reflections: Blue Rock Mennonite Congregation 1966-1991.* Blue Rock Mennonite School Research Project, 1991.

Shirk, Joseph S. and Ezra S. Zimmerman, *Records of the Old Order Mennonites from 1750 to 1963.* New Holland and Ephrata, Pa.: The Authors, [1963].

Statement of Christian Doctrine and Rules and Discipline of the Conservative Mennonite Churches of York and Adams County Pennsylvania, n.p., 1974.

Statement of Christian Doctrine and Rules and Discipline of the Eastern Pennsylvania Mennonite Church and Related Areas, n.p. 1993.

Statement of Christian Doctrine and Rules and Discipline of the Hope Mennonite Fellowship, n.p., 1987.

Statement of Faith of the Southeastern Mennonite Conference, n.p., 1991.

Statement of Faith and Practice of Sonlight Chapel, Maysville, Ohio. 1993.

Statement of Position on Divorce and Remarriage. Southeastern Mennonite Conference, n.p., 1983.

Statement on Inter-Mennonite Relationships. Irwin, Ohio: Conservative Mennonite Conference, 1992.

Stauffer, Enos E. *Die Briefe an David Stauffer.* Port Trevorton, Pa., 1990.

Stauffer, Enos E. *Uncle Aaron Stauffer's Diary 1947-1956.* Port Trevorton, Pa., 1995.

Stauffer, Enos. "Snyder County Old

Order Mennonite Ministers' List 1845-." *Historical Center Echoes* 16 (January 1993): 7-9.

Stauffer, Jacob W. *A Chronicle or History Booklet About the So-Called Mennonite Church*. Translated by Amos B. Hoover. Lancaster, Pa.: Lancaster Mennonite Historical Society, 1992. Originally published in German in 1855.

Stauffer, John L. *Godward or Worldward, Which?* Harrisonburg, Va.: Christian Light Publications, n.d.

Stauffer, John L. *Why Should Christians Wear Distinctive Attire?* Crockett, Ky.: Rod and Staff Publishers, n.d.

Stotzfus, Grant M. *Mennonites of the Ohio and Eastern Conference*. Scottdale, Pa.: Herald Press, 1969.

Stauffer, Louella. *Record of Members of the Stauffer Mennonite Church at the Present Time, 1990*. Gordonville, Pa.: Gordonville Print Shop, 1990.

Sword and Trumpet. Harrisonburg, Va.: *Sword and Trumpet*, 1929- .

Ulle, Robert F. "Origins of the Stauffer (Pike) Mennonite Church." *Pennsylvania Mennonite Heritage* 9. (July 1986): 18-23.

Umble, John S. "Extinct Mennonite Churches in Ohio," *Mennonite Quarterly Review*, 18 (Jan, Jul, Oct 1944), 19 (Jan, Jul 1945), 20 (Jan 1946).

The Unity and Purity of the Church. Lancaster, Pa.: The Reformed Mennonite Church.

Weaver, Martin G. *Mennonites of Lancaster Conference*. Scottdale, Pa.: Mennonite Publishing House, 1931.

Weiler, Lloyd M. "An Introduction to Old Order Mennonite Origins in Lancaster County Pennsylvania:

1893-1993." *Pennsylvania Mennonite Heritage* 16 (October 1993):2-13.

Weiler, Lloyd M. "Historical Overview of Weaverland Conference Origins," in *Directory of the Weaverland Conference Mennonite Churches 1995*. Womelsdorf, Pa.: Ruth A. Wise, 1995.

Wenger, A. Grace. *Frontiers of Faithfulness: The Story of the Groffdale Mennonite Church*. Leola, Pa.: Groffdale Mennonite Church, [1992].

Wenger, John C. *Faithfully Geo. R.: The Life and Thought of George R. Brunk I*. Harrisonburg, Va.: Sword and Trumpet, 1978.

Wenger, John C.. *History of the Mennonites of the Franconia Conference*. Telford, Pa.: Franconia Mennonite Historical Society, 1937.

Wenger, John C.. "Jacob Wisler and the Old Order Mennonite Schism of 1872 in Elkhart County, Indiana." *Mennonite Quarterly Review* (April and July, 1959)

Wenger, John C.. *The Mennonite Church in America*. Scottdale, Pa.: Herald Press, 1966.

Wenger, John C.. *The Mennonites in Indiana and Michigan*. Scottdale, Pa.: Herald Press, 1961.

Wenger, John C.. *Separated Unto God*. Scottdale, Pa.: Mennonite Publishing House, 1951.

Wenger, John C.. *The Yellowcreek Mennonites*. Goshen, Ind.: Yellow Creek Mennonite Church, 1985.

Why Christian Women Wear the Headship Veiling. Crockett, Ky.: Rod and Staff Publishers, 1983.

Wiesel, Barbara Bowie. *From Separatism to Evangelism: A Case Study of Social and Cultural Change Among the Franconia Conference

Mennonites, 1945-1970. University of Pennsylvania, Ph.D., 1973.

Yoder, Arletha Zehr Bender. *The History of Hope Mennonite Fellowship in Pennsylvania*. Bethel, Pa.: Little Mountain Printing, 1994.

Yoder, Elmer S. *The Beachy Amish Mennonite Fellowship Churches*. Hartville, Ohio: Diakonia Ministries, 1987.

Yoder, Elmer S. and Jewel Showalter. *We Beheld His Glory, Rosedale Bible Institute The First Forty Years: 1952-1992*. Irwin, Ohio: Rosedale Bible Institute, 1992.

Yoder, Elmer S. and Paton Yoder. *The Hartville Amish and Mennonite Story 1905-1980*. Hartville, Ohio: Knowles Press, 1980.

Yoder, Nate. "Mennonite Fundamentalism Revisited after Marsden." *Mennonite Historical Bulletin* 52 (October 1992): 1-5.

Zimmerman, Elsie. "Old Order Mennonite Weddings." *Historic Schaefferstown Record* 21 (April, 1987): 19-43.

Index

About the Author

Stephen E. Scott grew up in southwestern Ohio. He attended the Beavercreek Township schools, Cedarville College, and Wright State University. During a time of spiritual seeking, he attended many "plain" churches, including a variety of conservative Mennonite churches. Scott lived in the Amish and Mennonite community in Holmes County, Ohio, for a year. In 1969 he attended the Numidia Mennonite Bible School in Pennsylvania and the same year began two years of alternate service at Lancaster Mennonite High School in Pennsylvania. During this time, Scott joined the Old Order River Brethren Church, one of the conservative Anabaptist groups. In 1973 he married Harriet Sauder. The Scotts have three children and live near Columbia, Pennsylvania.

In 1979-80 he taught at Clearview Mennonite School. Since 1984 Scott has worked as a researcher and writer for Good Books and The People's Place in Intercourse, Pennsylvania. He has written *Plain Buggies*, *Why Do They Dress That Way*, *The Amish Wedding and Other Special Occasions of the Old Order Communities*, and *Amish Houses and Barns*. He is also the coauthor of *Living Without Electricity*.